AF594123

SUCCESS MOTIVATION®

THE STORY OF PAUL J. MEYER

THE MILLION DOLLAR PERSONAL SUCCESS PLAN

By: Lois S. Strain
and Gladys W. Hudson

Library of Congress Cataloging-in-Publication Data

Library of Congress Cataloging-in-Publication Data

Strain, Lois Smith.
The story of Paul J. Meyer.

1. Meyer, Paul J. 2. Businessmen—Biography.
3. Success in business. I. Hudson, Gladys W. II. Title.
HF5386.S8832 1987 338'.04'0924 [B] 86-29525
ISBN 0-8119-0720-1

International Standard Book Number: 0-8119-0720-1
Library of Congress Catalog Card Number: 86-29525

For information address:
Frederick Fell Publishers, Inc.
2131 Hollywood Boulevard
Hollywood, Florida 33020

MANUFACTURED IN THE UNITED STATES OF AMERICA

1 2 3 4 5 6 7 8 9 0

THE STORY OF
PAUL J. MEYER

ACKNOWLEDGEMENTS

Preparing the manuscript for this book has been an unusually enjoyable and exciting experience. Perhaps the most memorable aspect of the project has been the opportunity to know better a number of people who have provided information for various portions of the work.

Our grateful appreciation goes to Paul J. Meyer for his cooperation at every stage of the project. He gave many hours to interviews about his early experiences, and opened his files to provide career information and records, and shared letters and photographs from family sources.

People in all of the companies that make up the SMI family of companies have been helpful in providing information and insights into the personality and activities of Meyer. SMI distributors and clients all over the world have responded to requests for information. Without their help, our task would have remained incomplete.

Gladys W. Hudson
Lois S. Strain
Waco, Texas

January, 1987

TABLE OF CONTENTS

CHAPTER 3: GAINING MATURITY

CHAPTER 4: WINDS OF CHANGE

CHAPTER 5: THE DREAM

CHAPTER 6: SMI AROUND THE WORLD

CHAPTER 7: THE LENGTHENED SHADOW

CHAPTER 8: RELATIONSHIPS

CHAPTER 9: AS A MAN THINKETH. . .

FOREWORD

Paul J. Meyer is the kind of person who makes achievement look easy. When you know his full story, however, it becomes obvious that what he has done to achieve outstanding results is the same thing others can do: he has used his God-given talents and abilities to their maximum potential, and he has pursued challenging goals with dedication and commitment.

I have known Paul J. Meyer for more than thirty years—in times of prosperity, and in adversity. I have watched him grow in business and professional expertise and in the Christian graces. The philosophy of life described by the Apostle Paul is descriptive also of this latter day Paul: "I have learned to find resources in myself whatever my circumstances. I know what it is to be brought low, and I know what it is to have plenty. I have been thoroughly initiated into the human lot with all its ups and downs—fullness and hunger, plenty and want. I have strength for anything through Him who gives me power." (Phillippians 4:11–13 NEB)

The most remarkable achievement of this unusual man has been the building of a company based on an altruistic dream to share with as many people as possible a vision of the potential that is God's gift to every human being. He has pursued that dream with single-minded courage and unflagging energy.

The business success that Paul J. Meyer has enjoyed has provided him with the means for various approaches to achieving his goal to help people discover their full potential. His gifts of money, time and effort, and his unselfish leadership have produced a significant impact on a number of organizations for youth, for Christian training, and for other community causes. Although his monetary gifts have been generous, his time, energy and organizational ability have made even more important contributions than the dollars themselves.

Underlying all of his activities are a strong foundation of Christian values and the determination to be all that God has made it possible for him to be.

The story of Paul J. Meyer will inspire you to discover and use more of your own potential to reach the goals that are important to you—to make your life count for more.

William M. (Bill) Hinson
Baylor University

January, 1987

CHAPTER ONE

AS THE TWIG IS BENT

Whatever you
vividly imagine,
ardently desire,
sincerely believe,
and enthusiastically
act upon

must inevitably
come to pass.

Paul J. Meyer

CHAPTER ONE

AS THE TWIG IS BENT

PICTURE OF A SUCCESSFUL ENTREPRENEUR

Paul J. Meyer, just past the mid-century mark, looks more like a movie star than a business tycoon. Of medium stature and athletic build, he is suave and personable. Penetrating dark eyes, softened by innate courtesy, assess the visitor. A voice devoid of regionalism, expresses cordial welcome. Even the casual stranger realizes at once that the man likes people—there is a dynamism in his attitude, a warmth in his ready smile, and a youthful vigor implying that the silver that has almost completely obscured the formerly dark color of his hair is premature.

Abundant energy, enthusiasm, intensity, and a genuine concern for others vie for ascendancy in his nature. In conversation, his alertness keeps him a step ahead, and one feels his sense of urgency, a force that sometimes develops into impatience with the trivial. Self-confident, yet ever eager to learn more, he has insatiable curiosity. A man with strong convictions about the verities of life, his priorities are sound, his faith in himself remains unshaken, and his belief in the goodness of others approaches the naive. Just what makes this man tick?

Although Paul Meyer is definitely in step with today, with his eyes focused on tomorrow, he is firmly anchored in his past. His phenomenal memory is bolstered by carefully preserved records of his year-by-year personal and business life in a series of organized files in his office. His eyes twinkle as he recalls amusing incidents and then turn provocatively piercing as he reflects upon unfortunate incidents that others usually label failures—though he calls them "temporary setbacks." And he is quick to say that those setbacks have been valuable learning experiences for him. With the acumen of a critic, he assesses his own life.

ROOTS

Paul Meyer's roots go back to his maternal grandmother, Margaret Weems Dow, born in Edinburgh, Scotland, in 1863—a child of the heather, imbued with Scottish lore and a love for the highlands and moors—as well as Princess Street and "the Royal Mile." Yet she dreamed of a world beyond her homeland. Eagerly she welcomed family plans to go to the "New World." Because visas were not available for the brood to enter the United States, they went first, in June, 1889, to Canada—Peterborough, Ontario. In December of that same year, Margaret married Adam B. Rutherford who was born in Canada in 1856—also of Scotch parentage. Soon after they married, they moved to Kalamazoo, Michigan. Paul's grandfather, Adam Rutherford, cleared forty acres of rocky land in the beautiful wooded hills just outside the village of Kalamazoo that had been founded in 1829. Here the family lived for fifty years, growing corn and raising animals. Paul recalls going there for a visit when he was five years old and being enthralled with the animals—horses, cattle, and hogs. His grandfather, with back-breaking diligence, had cleared the land, and in old-world tradition, used the stones from the land to build a sturdy six-foot rock fence encircling the entire forty acres. In 1951 after an uncle's death, the ancestral farm was offered to Paul for $8,000. He declined the offer, for even then he was a discerning young man. His reason was simple. "It looked like the grapes of wrath and had the worst soil in the United States!"

On this farm Paul's mother, Isabelle Rutherford, was born in 1890. Near here she was schooled and trained by conscientious, devout parents. About her mother, Isabelle said, "To those in need, she gave; to those in sickness, she ministered; and she was mid-wife for every child born within twenty miles! In fact she was 'head honcho' at the Congregational church, at the school, and with the farmers. Actually, she was the matriarch of that Michigan county."

With such an example, it is easy to see why her daughter became a nurse, eventually serving as head nurse at Michigan's renowned Bronson Hospital—some thirty miles south of Battle Creek. Ever an avid reader and a dedicated student, she eventually chose to leave the nursing profession, go back to school and prepare for teaching. Hospital work allowed her to help mend bodies, but teaching gave her the opportunity to guide, to influence, to challenge young people—to build both minds and souls.

On a vacation visit to her sister in California, this personable, attractive young woman met August Carl Meyer. Both in their early thirties, they found that they had much in common—primarily their European heritage. Meyer came from Colmar, Germany—in the Haut-Rhine Department. With national pride, he told of his continental background. Rich in world history, Colmar was "a free imperial city" in 1226, then fell under the Swedes from 1632–34, the French in 1697, the Germans in 1871, the French again in 1919, then the Germans again in 1940 during World War II, and finally was retaken by the French in February 1945. When Carl Meyer was born, Colmar, overcoming its turbulent past, had become a bustling manufacturing city. For fifty years Carl's father was chief engineer on the same train between Strasborg, France, and Frankfurt, Germany.

Young Carl Meyer learned cabinet-making from a master craftsman of the Black Forest who produced exquisitely hand-carved pieces. An elaborately carved headboard of rosebuds and wreaths supplied Meyer with sufficient funds to come to America when he was twenty-eight. His decision to seek his fortune in the United States was encouraged by his father. Both recognized the inevitability of political unrest that was to embroil Europe for years yet to come. Carl also yearned for the freedom to be his own man, to earn his living with the skill of his hands, and to be the master of his own destiny. He believed that America was the true land of opportunity. This creative, self-confident, five-foot-seven young man with a slight limp (from a childhood fall from a horse) arrived in Brooklyn, New York, in 1920, knowing not a soul. Immediately he secured a job in the shipyards. Lacking a knowledge of English, young Meyer found communication with his co-workers a problem; he was often teased and frequently the butt of jokes. One he always recalled—the time his co-workers put white paint in his milk-thermos!

Constantly looking for greener pastures, the young man moved down to the South Carolina shipyards for a stint as a carpenter before he heard "the California call." It took him a year to cross the United States to California, working at odd jobs *en route*. Isabelle's sister and her husband lived in California, and Carl was hired by the husband, Fred Rinkert, to work as a carpenter. He brought both old-world

EACH OTHER

Though we search the world for friends,
Seeking pleasure, though we wander,
Happiness begins and ends
Here at home, not over yonder.

Fame may come, or fortune smile,
But we always learn, my brother,

All we have in life worth while
Is each other.

Not so long the life of man,
Not so strong the fragile tether;
Let us spend the time we can,
All the time we can, together.

Brother, sister, daughter, son,
Wife or husband, father, mother—
These our wealth, our only one,
Just each other

Douglas Malloch

craftsmanship and creativity to the job. His genius for design, invention, and experimentation stood him in good stead—all qualities destined to be transmitted to his son. It was through the Rinkerts that Isabelle, during a visit to their home, met Carl Meyer.

Romance blossomed between Isabelle Rutherford and Carl Meyer although previously Isabelle had been too deeply dedicated to her career to give any consideration to marriage. In addition, Carl Meyer was a Lutheran and she was a Congregationalist! Nevertheless, within three weeks they were married! The first abode of the couple was a tent, in which they lived for six weeks, for they were unable to find a house in Campbell, California. Carefully preserved by son Paul is a picture of that tent of 1923.

As Paul Meyer reflects upon his heritage, he is quick to credit his parents for their influence on his life. His German father taught him precision, resourcefulness, creativity, inventiveness. "He could start with *nothing* and make anything," his son averred. "And mother was a saint!"

When Carl Meyer immigrated to the United States, he severed all ties with the Old World, never going back; so Paul never knew his paternal grandparents. But one of Carl's four sisters came to live in San Francisco. She visited the hospital on the day of Paul's birth and left a framed poem, *The Only Thing We Have in Life Is Each Other,* remarking that the message seemed to apply to Paul's parents. Unwittingly, she made a casual remark about the baby's big ears. The father was so upset that he ordered his sister to leave and never spoke to her again. 'The hammer was down!" Although she lived out her life in San Francisco and he lived in San Jose, only forty miles apart—the only two of the family in the States—they never spoke again. After he was seventy, Carl feverishly tried to locate his sister, but his efforts were futile. His disappointment confirmed his belief that he had been right to break old ties. And just before his death, he extracted a promise from his wife that she would not pursue or search for information about his family in Germany, and her promise was kept.

CHILDHOOD MEMORIES

Paul Meyer's stoic, determined father left an indelible influence on his sons. "Because he believed that you could start with nothing and make anything, he showed us how to be inventive. He went to

Isabelle and Carl Meyer.

Paul Meyer—a very young ball player.

The first home for Isabelle and Carl Meyer.

elaborate ends to teach his children how to survive—to have a trade," Paul recalled, "and the bicycle story is a good illustration. I wanted a bicycle, as most youngsters do. So we went to the junk yard and found a wrecked bike. I was about eleven then. We took the thing apart. He showed me how to re-spoke the wheels and to buy the necessary parts. Then we stripped it of paint and rebuilt it all the way up."

The youth was exultant; his pride in his bike was boundless; not only did he have a fine bike—but he had played a significant role in its quality. Consequently, during the next three years he exploited this initial venture. Father and son built a lye-bath in the backyard—a pit about 3′ × 5′. In it Paul stripped over three hundred bikes, then repaired, repainted, and sold them. A 6′ × 4′ foot *Bicycle Repair* sign on Shelley Avenue in Campbell, California, brought in the business. Paul canvassed the older sections of town for used bikes, and even his mother was coerced into taking in old bikes at the door. Then Paul rebuilt them at night. This part-time business continued from Paul's twelfth to his sixteenth year.

With such valuable background experience, young Paul was ready for advancement. Like most juveniles, he wanted a car. He had made *real* money in the bicycle reclamation business—why not do the same with a car? He and his father made another trip to the junk yard where they found a "wreck" for a few dollars. They had it towed home, spread a big canvas in the backyard, and took the wreck apart. "If you can put the thing together so it will run, you can have it," said the father. The boy accepted the challenge with excitement. He worked endless hours on the project with the help and encouragement of his father. He cut down the body of the old Studebaker and made a pick-up which the pair drove for several years.

These successful ventures led the Meyers to the construction of a new home—the whole thing, including the plumbing, the electrical wiring—everything except the tile floor. The elder Meyer was the original "do-it yourself" individual. Said his son Paul, "Why, he wouldn't even buy a can of colored paint—he always mixed his own colors. His motivation was to teach us. I remember one time when I bought a model airplane. When I brought it home, he took it away from me. 'Design your own!' he demanded."

That was the challenge. Paul studied, experimented and produced. Soon he was winning all of the model airplane contests in the county. Photos in the family album show an impressive fleet of radio-controlled planes with seven-foot wingspan and the awards they brought.

Desire is the
dynamic motivation
behind every
worthwhile purpose.

Desire is the
inspiration that keeps
the flame of
progress burning.

Paul J. Meyer

But the youth's pride in winning any contest rested in the knowledge that he had done the construction himself—"from scratch." The creativity of designing something new and then bringing it into reality became a life-long challenge for Paul. He didn't—and still doesn't—want boxed "ready-to-be-put-together" planes—or plans. He wanted to design his own. If he ran into a problem, he went to a hobby shop and asked questions. He learned early to seek advice from experts—and the library. "I learned that you can find out almost anything if you just ask." The result of Paul's model plane expertise was far more than his bedroom ceiling full of suspended planes. He still draws on his ability to visualize something new, figure out how to do it, learn what he needs to know, and then bring the project to completion.

Throughout the years Paul has preserved a letter he and his brother Carl received from their father, who was away on a trip, when Paul was about twelve:

> Hello Carl and Paul my good sons, I have a little job you both can do for me. It is easy if you just follow my steps from here on. Get a 1 × 3 about 20 ft. long or nail 2 pieces together—maybe Mr. Belding can get it for you—just long enough to reach from the top of chimney to the bottom. Tack or tie 1 or 2 socks on the end, but not bigger than the opening in the chimney. Swing yourself up the roof in stocking feet, make along ridge one foot on each side of ridge so that roofing won't break, then run the rod with sock *slowly* down the flue and slowly up again several times, giving the soot a chance to fall *down.* Don't pull the soot out on top, let it fall down, work slow and take your time, also pull stove pipe out and stuff with rags or paper first. After the soot has settled then take paper out on bottom and clean out by hand in a bucket very slowly, and before you put the furnace pipe back, see if there is excessive soot in it. If so then it should be cleaned also. Get your job laid out first, prepare everything before you start, then do your job. Do it carefully like I would, take precaution so no one gets hurt unnecessarily. I know you can do it. See that all pipes are really good together again on account of fumes. Well, it's as good as done, I know that.

The truck Paul and his father built from salvaged parts.

Isabelle Rutherford Meyer

August Carl Meyer

Parents of Paul Meyer

These directions were accompanied by a sheet of detailed drawings, with the admonition: "Do it whenever you think you can." This in itself was sufficient challenge! The boys knew that "whenever you think you can" meant any time between now and and the time their Dad returned home!

Paul recalls the German obsession for exaction exemplified in his father. Just before leaving on a trip, Paul's father directed him to put up a fence down the side of the family property, stating that he would be drastically penalized if the posts were not exactly in line.

Paul's job was to dig the holes, set the posts, and stretch the wire. The youth, with some fear and trembling but determination, completed the task, and even years later delighted in "showing off" the perfection of his post line-up.

A similar experience involved a gas line from the family home to the street—about two hundred feet. The father insisted that the ditch be square. Paul was using a round-headed shovel; so he asked why the ditch had to be square. "Just as discipline!" curtly replied the father. Fifteen-year-old Paul rebelled and said that he wasn't going to do it, and furthermore, "I will never make my living with my hands," he added. This decision is one he has kept. He works hard—harder even than many of his associates realize—but always with his head, not his hands. He has retained much of his father's desire for perfection but has learned to temper the demand for perfection with practicality. If a "square" ditch is necessary, he demands it; but if a rounded one will achieve the desired purpose, he can accept—sometimes grudgingly—a subordinate's choice to make it that way.

Some time later came another memorable experience. Paul won an award at school for making a magazine rack in woodshop. When his father returned from a three-month trip, the boy pocketed his modesty, showed his father the award and relayed the extravagant praises of the teacher, who had declared it the best executed work that he had seen in his classes. The father examined it carefully, then began his critical remarks. Paul listened quietly, took the rack to the garage, picked up an ax and demolished his creation. One exhibit from the woodwork class escaped, however—a footstool which the proud mother carefully preserved for many years.

Paul remembers his father as a mechanical and electrical genius who expected perfection from others. Paul lived up to those expectations in some ways; his diligence brought him an *A* in mechanical drawing and house plans. He preserved the results of his efforts in

THE MILLION DOLLAR PERSONAL SUCCESS PLAN

by *Paul J. Meyer*

FOUNDER & CHAIRMAN OF THE BOARD
SMI INTERNATIONAL, INC.
WACO, TEXAS

I-Crystallize Your Thinking

Determine what specific goal you want to achieve. Then dedicate yourself to its attainment with unswerving singleness of purpose, the trenchant zeal of a crusader.

II-Develop a Plan for Achieving Your Goal, and a Deadline for Its Attainment

Plan your progress carefully: hour-by-hour, day-by-day, month-by-month. Organized activity and maintained enthusiasm are the well-springs of your power.

III-Develop a Sincere Desire for the Things You Want in Life

A burning desire is the greatest motivator of every human action. The desire for success implants "success consciousness" which; in turn, creates a vigorous and ever-increasing "habit of success."

IV-Develop Supreme Confidence in Yourself and Your Own Abilities

Enter every activity without giving mental recognition to the possibility of defeat. Concentrate on your strengths, instead of your weaknesses...on your powers, instead of your problems.

V-Develop a Dogged Determination to Follow Through on Your Plan, Regardless of Obstacles, Criticism or Circumstances or What Other People Say, Think or Do

Construct your Determination with Sustained Effort, Controlled Attention, and Concentrated Energy.

OPPORTUNITIES never come to those who wait...they are captured by those who dare to ATTACK.

drawings, but he threw the mechanical drawing tools in the trash can, vowing never to use such tools again as long as he lived. Yet in retrospect, the son admits that there was value in the discipline: "That's where I got the idea for Point Five of the *Million Dollar Personal Success Plan"*—develop a dogged determination to achieve your goals."

Written when Meyer, at age nineteen, began selling insurance, the *Million Dollar Personal Success Plan* formed the basic concept for programs later produced for Success Motivation Institute. "I learned a great deal from my father," Paul says. "He taught me the use of my hands—how to make anything that you can visualize. . . creativity. He also taught me the merit of work and patience and pride and organization. These lessons can be hard—but profitable," reflected Paul. "Then there was another principle my father stressed over and over—relate the normally unrelated. He taught us how to visualize combinations of ideas. My brother Carl used this principle of combining ideas when he developed the innovative Aqua Slide and Dive products that he designed and markets throughout the world."

A warm smile surfaces when Paul Meyer, the hard-nosed businessman, is asked about his mother. "She believed in people. Her credo was to remember the good and forget the bad. To her, there weren't any *bad* people. Even the worst were ninety percent good, she thought—maybe just unfortunate. She was a devout Congregationalist."

Family-centered memories are multiple for Paul Meyer. "I remember well the Victory Garden we had during World War II. It was Number One in the county. Not only was the lay-out of the garden perfect, but so was plant alignment. The plants dared not waver from the straight line. A taut string had been used at planting time, and if any seed sprouted out-of-line, the young plant was yanked out. Gravel pathways ran between the rows." The Meyer garden was a productive showplace. Precision and discipline paid off.

The family's preparation for the construction of a barbecue pit and a fish pond took over a year. Just the right rocks had to be collected, for the finished product was ever in the mind of the builders. "The dream must proceed the actuality," the man continually told his sons.

The great father-son conflict between Paul and the elder Meyer was openly expressed in the father's attitude toward sports. "They're a waste of time—fruitless!" the man would say in exasperation. Yet Paul, like most healthy adolescents, was stimulated by the exercise and the competitive spirit; and he excelled, for he had been taught that anything worth doing was worth doing well. He became a star on the high school basketball team. Although the father tolerated participation in practice, when the championship game came up, he told Paul—for some reason no one will ever know—that he could not go. And Paul knew that his father would never retract his decision. But this time fate intervened in an unexpected way. Brother Carl, feeling the injustice of the situation, acted spontaneously. He tried to argue Paul's case and found himself suddenly embroiled in physical combat with his father. In the course of the scuffle, Carl pushed his father through the front window of the living room and continued the fight in the front yard. But during the melee he pitched Paul the car keys. Carl, Jr., was a young iron-man with a sense of justice—and a large measure of the father's own determination.

The game! Paul controlled his emotions and concentrated on the matter at hand; his team won the game. Yet there was a latent anxiety about returning home—he was tense. He entered the house quietly, saying not a word. Neither did his father speak. Nor did he comment on the newspaper's glowing report of the team's victory—if, indeed, he even read it. He isolated himself completely from his son's athletic prowess.

BOY SCOUTS

One activity to which Paul's father gave his support was scouting, and Paul recalls with affection Bernard Watson and Charlie Simonds—both dedicated Scout Masters who guided him through the essential progressive steps in scouting. "And we built our own scout hall," Paul declared with almost juvenile pride. Paul's recounting of how the scout hall was built also shows more than a trace of the juvenile love of taking a risk involving a bit of mischief that the boys justified by pointing to their admirable purpose. A group of the scouts, with Paul as one of the leaders in the ploy, attended a meeting of the Dad's Club that sponsored the troop. They explained that the makeshift arrangement for a meeting place was hampering their activities, and they asked their fathers to build them a scout hall. The boys, of course, were willing to help. The fathers, however, said they had no money available for such a project—even though they did agree that there was a valid need.

But Paul had learned well a lesson from his own father: don't be discouraged by obstacles. Find a way! So Paul had a plan. With the full knowledge of his troop leader, he organized the other boys and they made signs. At the next Dad's Club meeting, the boys showed up with their signs declaring that loving fathers would help their sons build a scout hall, and then marched around the room—then out. Paul's love of fun shows through as he tells how he minimized the risk to himself. He made sure that the scout's campaign took place while his own father was out of town. He figured that any repercussions would be over by the time he had to answer for his part in the demonstration.

At the next scout meeting, the Dad's Club met with the boys. They said they had been able to acquire three old houses that were to be demolished. They promised that if the boys would tear down the houses, remove all the nails and stack the lumber, they would help them build a scout hall from the salvage. The boys eagerly accepted the challenge, and the scout hall they built was a source of pride because they had invested something of themselves in it.

> "It was in scouting that I really found out how much I loved climbing ladders or setting goals—through the progressive realization of being a Tenderfoot, then Second Class, First Class, Star, Life and Eagle. A combination of what my dad taught me and the Scouts—that's how I acquired many of the basic ideas for Success Motivation Institute. Those scouting days included some of the happiest days of my life and one of the saddest."

On a special outing, a tragic incident left an indelible memory with the boy. His scout troop had joined 3,000 other scouts for a camporee at Santa Rosa, California. Paul and the Billy Farnham, son of the scoutmaster, shared a pup tent. The tent caught fire and the other boy died. The effect upon young Paul was traumatic. He told his scout master that he intended to become an Eagle Scout for them both. This goal was achieved, and throughout the years Paul has been faithful to this youthful vow in his dedication and exemplary support of the Boy Scouts.

A snapshot of Paul at salute in scout uniform has its place in the family photo album. His brother Carl became the first Eagle Scout in the county, and Paul the second. This achievement was one of the few

Paul as a Boy Scout.

Paul and his trumpet.

Paul's school picture.

that brought an expression of paternal approval. Not only did the father attend the award ceremony, but he gave Paul a crisp twenty dollar bill. The money seemed a fortune to the young man, for times were difficult and he knew that his father's earnings were only about thirty-five dollars a week. Although the father had pride in the achievements of his children, he was reluctant to admit it to *them.* The perceptive mother tried to explain to Paul when he complained that nothing he did ever pleased his father. "You know, your father spends all his time going around bragging about you."

Paul's father loved his children, but he lacked the ability to verbalize his feelings or to demonstrate his affection openly. Perhaps he felt that demonstrating affection might be considered a sign of weakness, or perhaps he feared that compliments would have a deleterious effect on the recipient. Later when Paul broke physical fitness records in the Army, he sent newspaper clippings reporting the facts to his parents. The father's response was "Don't you have anything to say besides bragging?" Yet Paul's mother later confided that her husband carried the news clippings in his billfold until they were barely readable.

The Meyer boys were not alone in the ability to use their creativity and imagination. Their sister Elizabeth, the middle child in the family, possessed the same desire to excel and to achieve that the brothers developed. She not only acquired homemaking skills from her mother, but she worked right alongside the boys in the fields and fruit orchards. She became an excellent cook and an accomplished seamstress. She even learned to make men's suits and upholster furniture. Elizabeth also learned to place a high value on friendships. By the time she started to school, she had become part of a group of girls whose friendship has lasted half a century. The six friends lived in the same neighborhood, went through school together, and shared all their activities. Isabelle served as a mentor for the group, a second mother to Elizabeth's friends. The six friends have maintained an intimate friendship throughout their adult lives, and the five who survive today still live in the same community.

THE YOUNG ENTREPRENEUR

From early childhood Paul had an insatiable drive, not only to surpass the records of others, but to outstrip his own records as well. "I had a

Setting the record—101 boxes of prunes.

Paul the weight lifter.

Paul picking apricots for his mother.

magazine route when I was twelve or thirteen and I broke the national records selling *Liberty Magazine* and the *Ladies Home Journal.*"

Paul's prune-picking experiences further proved his prowess. Some three weeks at the last of July and the first of August is "prune time" in California. The youngster participated in the harvest from the time he was six until he was sixteen years old. Migrant workers were the usual laborers. One day young Paul called the local newspaper to inquire about the record for prune-picking. Nobody had ever picked sixty lugs of prunes in one day. Passing the mark became the boy's goal.

"You picked up prunes on your hands and knees," recalled Paul. "I got up at two o'clock in the morning and went to the orchard. I hung a flashlight from a tree and unloaded a hundred of those big lug boxes and began to fill them—steadily." In his lengthened day the determined lad set a world record of 101 lugs of prunes—5,050 pounds gathered by one individual in one day! At "two-bits a lug," he earned over twenty-five dollars. Of course he was exultant as he compared that day's earnings to a week's income for the average worker in that difficult economy. When he reached home, his father was reading the newspaper, but the lad interrupted to tell of his accomplishment. All that Paul remembers is that his father lowered his paper and said with deliberation, "Don't tell me what you made today. Tell me how much of it you will have ten years from now and I'll tell you how much you made today."

The boy was infuriated by the "put-down." He went to his room and kicked the door shut. Soon his mother came in to soothe his disappointment, for she was ever the mediator. He began to think over his circumstances and recalled what his father had so often said about free enterprise: "Any time you learn something and teach it to somebody else, then pay them less than you get paid, the difference is your profit." He believed it would work for him in the prune business.

The next day Paul asked one of his teachers to help him draw up a simple contract, which he then mimeographed and used to recruit helpers. He signed up some forty boys to pick prunes under his contract. But only about half of them showed up for the first job. He soon learned to sign up about twice as many helpers as he needed, and even then some would leave because the work was hard. He and his crew worked right along with migrant workers. The boys were employed on a commission basis and he made a five-cent override on their work. From this amount, he had to pay people to shake the

A self-confident

attitude

is the most important

asset

you can possess.

Paul J. Meyer

trees, and he also had to keep the records on each worker, collect the wages due, and see that each one was properly paid. The orchard owner was pleased. The arrangement brought him much-needed labor and saved supervision and bookkeeping. Paul was learning fast.

"I remember working for a fellow named Beale, who was paying by the hour for picking apricots. I talked him into paying by the box. Soon I was making over a dollar and a half an hour. Then Beale got mad and fired me!"

Paul encountered the same situation hoeing around grape vines. The pay was fifty cents an hour. Paul asked the boss: "How many do you expect to be cultivated in an hour?" Then Paul contracted to work by the plant. Soon he was making well over a dollar an hour, and again he lost his job. Recalling these experiences, Paul Meyer becomes meditative. "You know, I've been fired from almost every job I've ever had until I started my own company. I was fired from all of them for being creative and innovative—striving as best I could to use all my potential."

It was not unusual for Paul to go to teachers and ask for their help or suggestions. He respected their judgment and was grateful for their help. He continued, as long as they lived, to correspond with Mrs. McCormick, his teacher in grades one through three; Mrs. Keesley, the fourth grade teacher; and Mrs. James, the fifth and sixth grade teacher. He still corresponds regularly with Bernard Watson, who was principal of his elementary school and Charles Simonds, principal of his alma mater, Campbell High School.

During the growing-up years, Paul sought a way to share with his father an open expression of their love for one another. He frequently expressed his sense of love for his father although Carl seemed able to express his feelings only in writing. Etched deeply in Paul's consciousness is his father-image overlaid with regrets and sorrow for their inability to communicate except for over 500 postcards his father sent him from 500 different towns in the United States. "I still have all of the postcards," said Paul, nostalgically. It was only in writing that his father could give free rein to his emotions.

Years later when Paul, at the age of twenty-one, had become the leading insurance agent in his area, he acquired some lots in Columbus, Georgia. His father was planning a visit, supposedly to buy Paul's car. Carl's hesitance about expressing his love for his children made it impossible for him to make a visit just to enjoy being with the family. Paul thought it would be an excellent plan for his father to build some small houses on the lots. It would be a source of profit for both him and his father. When Paul brought up the subject of the house construction, his father eagerly began to outline a plan for them to work together on the project. But Paul quickly let it be known that he didn't intend to help. In dismay, his father exclaimed, "You're not going to help me build them?"

"No, I sell life insurance," replied Paul. The pair argued the question angrily until the father stormed out of the house. The next day they met on the sidewalk in downtown Columbus. Neither said a word. Paul recalled, "I was going to make a call. I remember telling myself, 'I must be tough.' But I was hurting inside. When I went to make the sale, I was determined to succeed. I wouldn't have missed that sale for anything in the world. That prospect couldn't have escaped with a thousand *no's!*" Every additional attempt to establish a more loving relationship with his father seemed destined to fail, and he took his major satisfaction in life from exercising his capacity for success in other areas of life.

Although the son longed for a loving relationship, the father seemed unable to allow himself the freedom to experience that joy. Another time he came to visit Paul, this time to build an additional room on a house for Paul's father-in-law. Paul knew that his father had been *eyeing* a certain car—a 1953 Chevy; so he went out and bought the car, drove it home, and gave his father the keys, happy in the thought that he had found something he could do to show his love for his father. But he was disillusioned again.

"Who do you think you are, showing off, getting me a car?" In anger, the father rushed into the house, packed his bags, took his wife, and left. But he left in the new car!

Later Paul discussed the episode with his mother, for it was puzzling to him—as were most of his experiences with his father. The wise mother's comment was, "All he talked about on the way to California was the new car."

"But he's inconsistent!" replied Paul.

Paul was learning many things about human behavior and personality differences. One was that a young man who achieves remarkable success can be a threat to others and even an indictment to some. Success can be as difficult as failure, Paul concluded, for he loved his father.

As he analyzed the circumstances, Paul became more understanding. Evidence of the contrast in the father's life-style and his own were visible everywhere. Paul had built a spacious, elegant home with a screened-in swimming pool decorated with dozens of hanging orchid plants. He was the youngest member of the prestigious and highly publicized *Million Dollar Round Table* in the insurance world and had been the leading salesman in two insurance companies. Making money seemed to be the easiest thing he did. And with the abandon of youth, he spent it lavishly. He owned an eighty-two-foot yacht and several airplanes. No wonder a craftsman father of German extraction, whose pride was in the artistry of his hands, had difficulty in bridging the gap between the Old World concept of success and that of a budding American entrepreneur!

"I keep telling you that all I do I learned from you," Paul would tell his father.

"You're not doing *anything* you learned from me," would come the caustic reply. And Paul again recalled his father's oft-repeated maxim about the free enterprise system. Paul had internalized it!

It was in the father-son relationship that Paul early in life learned to transcend disappointment, disillusion, and bitterness. He loved his father and credits him for many valuable lessons learned at his feet. Paul's greatest regret is that his father's stern approach to parenting robbed the family of many of the simple joys of loving relationships.

At the mention of his mother, Paul's eyes soften. "She never raised her voice and I never heard her say an unkind word," declares her son. "She had a fine Christian heritage, through which she skillfully and devotedly combined faith and work. She exerted a strong influence on all of us—spiritual, physical, mental, social, and financial—almost without our realizing it at the time. It was by example."

So close were the ties between mother and son that he regularly corresponded with her once or twice a week for over twenty years. And she did the first research for Paul's innovative *Dynamics of Personal Motivation*—"over half of it," Paul declared with pride. Then with a slight smile of amusement he said, "As she grew older she continued to send me research on the subject. She read everything."

"My mother was like Gandhi—absolutely non-violent. Her friends, my teachers, the scoutmaster—all told me that my mother was the most Christ-like person they had ever known. And she always smiled—you couldn't make her *not* smile. When my father exploded or cursed, I would ask, 'Don't you want to say something?' Her quiet answer would be, 'I don't have anything to say.' 'Are you mad?' I'd ask, for I really couldn't understand her silence. 'No, I'm not mad,' would come her quiet, controlled answer. She was a true example of *positive* living; she looked to strengths instead of weaknesses."

Vividly Paul recalls a particular dinner that his mother had painstakingly worked all day to prepare as a special treat for the family. But the father, upset or angry about some incident unknown to the rest of the family, chose dinner time to vent his displeasure. He dumped the food into a napkin and tossed it out the back door. Paul waited for his mother's reaction. Her response to the childish display was, "Well, I feel sorry for him. You know he is spoiled; he had four older sisters."

"Why don't you throw a skillet?" came Paul's youthful query.

Her reply was often from the Bible under such circumstances, and this was no exception. "I've been married to him for thirty years and I have always turned my other cheek. It's a long way to *seventy times seven."* And she should know, thought Paul; but he grumbled, "I'd punch him in the nose!" Surprised, the mother responded, "Why, that's non-human!"

"My mother was a remarkable woman. Giving of herself was one of her virtues. She made all the presents she showered on relatives and friends, for she was artistic and skillful with needlework. And she was a leader in many community activities—at home, at church, at school. As a role model she exemplified the positive Christian attitude. In her work as a nurse, a homemaker, and a teacher she was a *caring* person who made life rich for others."

This noble woman maintained her stalwart courage until the end of her life. She never wanted to be the source of any worry or hurt for others. One night shortly before her death Isabelle reached for Paul's hand as he sat at her bedside in the hospital. "Paul," she said, "don't let them hook me up to things; let God make the decisions." Then a few days later she begged, "Don't let anybody come to see me at the hospital tomorrow, Paul" When he returned to the hospital after midnight, she was visibly weaker. He reported her condition to his brother and sister in Los Angeles. The beloved mother died at eleven o'clock the following morning, as if she had planned it so—at eighty years of age.

How different was the terminal illness of his father. "I saw my father become sicker and sicker, spending the last five years of his life in bed, taking thousands of shots of painkiller—an embittered man." From intimate first-hand experience Paul Meyer learned a cardinal value in life—the absolute necessity of forgiveness, not only to free the offender but to liberate the offended!

Years later, in a very personal, lengthy letter, written before dawn under a strange compulsion, Paul poured out to a beloved nephew what life has taught him about forgiveness. He recounts the story of his father, whom he saw lose friend after friend because of his inability to forgive and forget.

> A couple and their children would visit us intermittently over a period of six months or so. Then my father would decide that he didn't like them any more, and the visits would cease. The next year it would be another family, then another. If he found out that I still talked to the children of these families, he would say, "We don't talk to them any more."

But for young Paul, these admonitions were overshadowed by his mother's discerning assessment, "Don't look down on people—see their possibilities." Paul crystalized these object lessons into a basic principle for living: *forgive and free yourself*. Paul continued:

> We as human beings are unforgiving because of poor attitudes, ingratitude, bitterness, and self-centeredness. But forgiveness brings freedom—less tension, less anxiety, as well as greater happiness, and the ability to love; and it provides the real biggie—it releases guilt. It actually opens the channel to God.

That letter is the best sermon on forgiveness one could desire, for its premises are rooted in personal experience.

The Meyer family album reveals some interesting history of the family, including the father's progressive construction of the spacious clapboard family home, as well as a picture of the school the children attended. By 1935, Paul had been photographed to display his first wristwatch, and in 1938, his first basketball. In 1940, he stands near a willow tree blowing his trumpet. Other interesting pictures are of Paul in a prize-winning Russian costume in 1942, as well as his photo in a Mexican costume, complete with hat and serape, and his eighth grade graduation pictures. By 1942, his brother Carl had advanced to riding a motor bike and was a proud member of Hi Y, and by 1945 Paul had a racing bike. Life became gradually more complex for the Meyer family.

But business acumen was not neglected by the Meyer boys. At an early age Paul became "hooked" on real estate. Even in his youth, he could see the potential increase in the value of well-located property—without the back-breaking expenditure of energy in prune-picking. By age fifteen, the boy had saved $2,500 of his hard-earned money. He found a piece of property "with a future, owned by a fellow who cut our hair," Paul recalled. His father refused to let him buy it. With bitter personal disappointment, Paul watched that property rise in value until it sold for $50,000. The seller then invested that money in 100 acres of land that some time later sold for a million dollars. Paul's instincts were right; and when he grew older, he followed them with remarkable success.

In 1946, young Paul Meyer was a graduate of Campbell High School with a creditable record, and he was in top physical shape because of his arduous weight-lifting program. Inducted that year at Camp Beale, California, he subsequently broke army physical fitness records for sit-ups, and "dips" or push-ups—3,500 at one time! He also recorded 81 one-arm pushups at one time! A picture of young Paul in swim trunks in November, 1946, at the barracks in South Carolina reveals his superb physical condition as he flexes his muscles. Stationed later at Fort Benning, Columbus, Georgia, he was immediately made a physical education instructor because of his physical expertise. He shattered all existing records in the Army's physical fitness test, scoring 495 out of the possible 500 points. Official records acclaimed him the most nearly perfect physical specimen in the history of the airborne forces.

It was parachuting that Paul found most exhilarating, for he was daring and self-confident. Stories around the camp declared that Paul *got rich* by substituting for reluctant recruits and collecting their jump pay at fifty dollars a jump!

Eighteen months later, after his discharge from the military, like many other young men, Paul turned to college. But his college life at San Jose College was brief—just ninety days. The pace was too slow for his inquiring mind. He had questions and he wanted answers—*now*. One day in his post-war class of some two hundred, he had the nerve to interject a question. The lecturer paused to say that the class was so large and the subject mass so comprehensive that he could not use class time for individual questions. No "rubber-stamp student" satisfied to follow a text and listen to sterile lectures in over-crowded classrooms, Paul complained to the dean. "If this is the way college works," he told the dean, "I can do it faster. Just give me a list of books to read, and I'll do it myself. I can get the answers I want that way." He concluded that he could do it on his own; and he became a "college drop-out."

This incident brought what was perhaps the severest criticism he ever received from his mother. Ever an advocate of education, Isabelle told her impatient son that he could not afford to be without the best possible education he could acquire. "You have two choices," she advised. "Either you go back to that college, eat crow, and ask to be reinstated, or exert a much greater effort and spend much more time to educate yourself." Reminiscent of his father's disciplined methods—and perhaps also of his father's stubborn determination to follow his own way—Paul began an intensive reading program that developed into a lifelong habit. Abetted by his innate curiosity and boundless energy in pursuit of whatever interests him, he has acquired a broad education, unlimited by the requirements and strictures of highly organized degree plans. Now he recognizes the wisdom of his mother's warning. He is quick to tell young people that an education is vital. In support of that belief, he has provided scholarships for a large number of young people who show evidence of the desire to develop their full potential. But he believes that an education should not end with a four-year college plan—it should be a constant, rewarding lifetime pursuit.

Paul's decision to leave college precipitated the necessity for new decisions. He had to make a living. That was the immediate challenge of his German heritage, and he was eager to meet it.

CHAPTER TWO
ESTABLISHING A CAREER

Decide what you want and write your goals.

Then convert your goals into positive, present tense statements called affirmations.

Affirm your goals each day until they become part of your subconscious mechanism.

Paul J. Meyer

CHAPTER TWO

ESTABLISHING A CAREER

PROFESSIONAL SELLING

Success did not come to Paul Meyer full-grown—like Diana on a seashell. There were times of crisis. He had decided at the age of sixteen that he wanted to make his living in professional selling. He recalled standing in the hot sun in a grape vineyard and vowing to himself that he would not spend his life in the type of work that had marked his early youth. But his concrete planning had not progressed beyond that point.

When Paul decided to leave college, he reviewed that previous resolution. There was only one question: "How do I get started?" The only person close to him who was involved in selling was his father-in-law, Mr. King; so Paul called Mr. King for advice. "I know you like to sell insurance, and I would like to try it, too," Paul told him. Then he asked if he should come back to Georgia. Mr. King agreed, but suggested that it would be much better if Paul planned to get a job with someone other than a relative.

Resolutely, Paul set out for Georgia. "How do I begin? What is the quickest road to the success I want?" he asked himself repeatedly. And overshadowing the present was always the tragic, inexplicable tent-fire death of his Boy Scout comrade! "Why him and not me?" There is a very serious, acute conscience in the Meyer make-up, as indicated by his reaction to this tragedy. Then after the military service had come his renunciation of the college pattern of training. He knew that he must depend upon his own resources. Although he did not yet have a clear picture of *how* he would do it, he fully expected to succeed in selling. After all, in his early youth he had won a national contest selling subscriptions to *Liberty* magazine and the *Ladies Home*

Journal. The love of competition and the fierce independent spirit that he had cultivated made selling an attractive challenge.

Post-war employment was at a desperate low. Paul faced a savagely competitive world, saturated with newly-discharged, seasoned veterans. Continually he recalled the paternal challenges of his childhood, "Meyers don't try; they *do!*" and, "The more you grow, the more possibilities you have." Then there was the athletic admonition, "I *expect* to win!" He was conditioning his mind and building the confidence necessary to win. And the young man needed that confidence. He had decided that his future lay in selling, even though he realized that "selling" involved far more than a salesperson and a product. He was convinced that it demanded both consummate skill in basic sales procedures and convincing integrity.

Youthful experience had taught him much about people and their motivation. Implicit in his make-up was his belief in people and their often latent potential—a belief instilled by his mother along with a generous spirit. His father had extolled the virtues of self-confidence, the setting of goals and the tenacity required to meet them. These attitudes formed the foundation of the young man's budding entrepreneurial ambitions, and his competitive spirit responded to the thrill of the chase.

He was ready to meet life head on—with courage and self confidence. His incisive review of his personal experiences led him to formulate the initial four steps of his succinct *Million Dollar Personal Success Plan.*

I. Crystallize your thinking.

II. Develop a plan for achieving your goal and a deadline for its attainment.

III. Develop a sincere desire for the things you want in life.

IV. Develop supreme confidence in yourself and your own abilities.

FOCUS ON INSURANCE

The post-war job market was highly competitive. Meyer called on fifty-seven insurance companies without getting a job! Finally, he was hired as a salesman for a life insurance company in Columbus,

Georgia. "And they fired me in three weeks because they said I was shy, introverted, possessing high mechanical aptitude—but not cut out for selling."

"I don't think your test showed everything. You're telling me I'm too quiet. You told me to ride out with some of your people, and I rode out with them; but I didn't say anything because I was listening. I can't learn anything while I'm talking," he told Mr. Clark.

"Then I assured him that I *could* sell—outsell his best people because they start too late and quit too early and take off too much time for coffee and lunch. The more I considered the situation, the more argumentative I became. I could make three times as many calls! And then I told Mr. Clark that the test doesn't show how hard a person will try or how much persistence he has. Well, he let me go—said he couldn't keep me because the home office had *X'd* it."

That evening, Paul mischievously told his father-in-law, "You had better give me a job, or I will have to move into your living room!" With a sly grin, Paul recalls, *"That* alerted him! It got his attention right away." For that reason—or some other—Mr. King did hire the young man to sell insurance for the largest exclusive weekly premium company in the nation.

Meyer's introduction to selling insurance was inauspicious, to say the least; but the young man had a sharp intellect and a determined spirit. His father-in-law presented him with a packet of information, and the company's superintendent, R.E. Stanley, drove him about four miles to the edge of town—in the black residential area. At that time life insurance agents sold to blacks or whites—never to both. "Mr. Stanley let me out of the car and handed me some applications and a sample life insurance policy. I asked if he intended to stay and help me. He said, 'No,' and drove off. I had never before seen an insurance policy of any kind. I went over and sat on a curb and read the policy. I stood up and looked around me. The neighborhood consisted of rows of identical shot-gun houses—so called because they were arranged one room right behind the other, providing a 'straight shot' from the front door right out the back. Since standing there didn't seem to be the way to accomplish anything, I went to the first house.

"A neat, mature black woman answered my knock. I took off my hat and told her my business—that this was the first house I'd called on and that I'd never sold any insurance in my life—that I'd never *seen* a policy before. She invited me in, we looked over the packet,

I would rather be a
master prospector
than to be a
wizard of speech
with no one
to tell my story to.

Paul J. Meyer

and she bought a policy. *My first sale!* Then I asked her who else would be interested. She took me next door and I (we?) sold another policy."

THE FIRST SUCCESS

Courtesy and honesty paid off. Paul trudged the four long miles home, but with renewed faith in himself. That first month he led the agency in sales of those weekly premium policies that brought in from 10¢ to 50¢ per week—which Paul quickly discovered he must collect personally!

Success continued. Paul recalls, "I sold more weekly premium insurance that year than anyone else had ever sold in the history of the company." People responded to a youth from California who took off his hat! At that time most Southern companies had one policy for white people with a cash value the second year and one for black people with a cash value the fourth year. But this company offered the same policy to black customers that others sold to white clients. This appealed to Paul's sense of justice—a trait he had learned from his mother. For two years he learned salesmanship in this first venture into the adult business world.

At the end of his first year with the weekly premium company—a year in which he led the company in sales—Paul went back to visit the office of the company that had let him go after a three-week trial. He recalls, "I doubled-parked on First Street, rode the elevator up four floors and handed Mr. Clark the bulletin telling of my sales record. I don't think he appreciated it." But it was the happy vindication of youth.

Although the youthful salesman had made an enviable record selling weekly premium insurance, he was eager to move up to selling ordinary or whole life insurance. This meant the premiums would be paid by the month or quarter and mailed to the company, freeing the agent's time for additional hours each week to sell. He kept his eyes open for an opportunity. It soon came with a relatively new company with headquarters in Atlanta, Georgia. Frank Caton had come from Atlanta to Columbus and stopped to see his friend Buddy Scott at the Buick agency. He asked if Buddy knew anyone who might be interested in working for his company in Columbus. Buddy looked up and saw Paul Meyer walking through the front door. "There's a guy," he told Caton, "just walking in. He's the best salesman I know."

The first house Paul built by selling insurance.

Paul's house trailer
that he named "Meyer's Mansion."

The Meyer brothers and sister:
Carl, Elizabeth, Paul.

"Buddy introduced us," Paul remembers. "Frank took me out to his car and showed me what he sold. It looked good to me, but I told him that he'd have to talk with my father-in-law, who was in the insurance business. 'Where does he work?' Frank asked.

"'Well,' I said, 'he's my boss.' Frank thought I'd lost my mind, but I told him, 'Mr. King looks out for my welfare; he doesn't care whether I work for him or not.' Then as soon as Mr. King and Mr. Caton saw one another's Shriner pins, all was well, and I went to work for Caton." That was March 6, 1950.

DISAPPOINTMENTS

But success in selling whole life insurance did not come quickly or easily for Paul. For the first nine months, he earned an average of $83.00 per month, but in the tenth month he earned $3,000, and the amount accelerated steadily from then on. That is a tribute to persistence! Paul is an adherent to the axiom, "Ninety percent of all failure comes from quitting."

Paul tells of the struggle to keep going throughout those discouraging days. "I was living in a one-bedroom apartment—and shared a kitchen and bathroom—for twenty-five dollars a month, and I was kicked out because I couldn't pay the rent in advance. But what I remember most is what I told the landlord—that whatever he did couldn't affect my attitude, that I considered myself rich—that I just didn't have things figured out yet, but when I did, I was going to be able to come back and buy this house—the whole block." What Paul realized, even though he didn't verbalize it, was this: "I have inner resources! I have faith in myself."

While he continued to struggle to maintain a home, Paul met Geneva Jones, who owned a trailer park in Columbus, Georgia. Her husband had died and she was managing the park. She loaned Paul fifty dollars for the down payment on a trailer—which he gave the high-sounding title of *Meyer's Mansion*. He took two spaces for the trailer, then put in a lawn out front and a fence on the sides, and his weights and barbells in the rear of the trailer. "I thought I was the richest guy in town!" he recalls. He still has the sign stored away as a reminder of the real values in life.

Possibly the hardest blow during this early period came when Paul had to sell his beloved barbells. As a youngster he had worked hard all one summer to buy the set. Now he had to part with it for ten dollars to make a payment to Mrs. Jones on the house trailer. Meeting his obligations was of primary importance.

As his skills improved and finances eased, Paul kept sight of the principle that material possessions are not the key to happiness—but that happiness stems from an innate temperament. He was making a comfortable living, but that was not enough. He wanted a challenge! And Paul soon found one!

It was at this time that young Meyer developed his carefully calculated telephone technique. Insurance sales, like many other types of selling, always depend on getting appointments with prospects in order to make presentations. Paul just couldn't seem to say the right words to convince a prospect that seeing him would be time well spent. One day he had spent several hours on the telephone. He had made more than fifty calls without succeeding in scheduling a single appointment. Late that evening, he sat on the steps of his house trailer, sunk in despair. So concerned was he that tears rolled down his cheeks, but giving up never occurred to him. Instead, he vowed that when he finally learned how to get appointments by telephone he would write out the technique and teach it to others who were experiencing the same frustration that was his. Necessity activated him and he responded to the challenge.

Paul began to plan carefully everything that he said to prospects on the telephone. He wrote out and tried various approaches. When one sentence worked, he marked it as a winner and used it again. A sentence, or a whole approach that didn't work was discarded. Painfully, step by step, he developed a winning technique. And he kept his vow. He wrote out his technique and later taught it to insurance salespeople when he was head of his own agency. He refined it still further as he established his own company, and it is still used and taught to SMI salespeople all over the world. Today, Paul still relies on his ability to get appointments by telephone as he calls on leading local and national figures in his efforts to gain support for the Boy Scouts, the Boys' Club, and other organizations that are a part of his community and world service.

At this critical stage in his professional development, there were only a few "how to" books on salesmanship available, but young Meyer with his usual acumen read them all. At the same time, he was busily crystallizing his own thoughts on the subject.

THE REWARDS OF PERSISTENCE

Eventually his persistence paid off. From that inauspicious beginning in 1950, he went on to lead the company in sales for three straight years. As a result, he was made a Vice President and Superintendent of Agencies. In testimony to his outstanding achievements, a number of major companies interviewed Paul in an attempt to recruit him. Royal entertainment, including penthouse dinners, was part of the pitch. But this prospective recruit was turned off when they pulled out the financial statement of his employer to compare with theirs; Paul believed—and still does—that the ethical approach to selling and recruiting is to present the benefits of your product or company—not to run down a competitor."

REVIVAL OF THE ENTREPRENEURIAL SPIRIT

True to his early training, Paul sought to preserve a portion of what he earned and to make it bring in added dividends. He set goals for earnings, savings, and investment. He was always on the lookout for a promising investment while he continued to concentrate 100% of his time and energy in his selling career. But he had the entrepreneurial spirit, and he invested in several "promising" businesses. Sometimes it turned out that the "promise" was largely in the imagination of the person who solicited his capital. He tells amusing stories about his early ventures and how he learned from these often bizarre enterprises.

When Paul was about twenty-one, he joined his father-in-law and a man who later became district attorney in that county to back a fellow in opening a bakery—$500 apiece—in Columbus, Georgia. He had visions of a nice little return on his investment. But disappointment was in store, Paul says. "As time passed, we had to continue putting money into the venture—it just wasn't making it. But we were being given bakery goods—the fellow would come by every few days and give me a loaf of bread.

"One day we decided that we'd gone far enough. I went by the bakery and found it closed, but I went around to the back because I had a key to the place. And I then discovered *why* it wasn't doing well. Our baker had set up housekeeping with a young woman who worked in the bakery. All his time and money had been going into that arrangement instead of into the business. I left to get a truck and remove the furniture, but when I returned, the couple had left, taking everything that wasn't nailed down. I did retrieve the counter and the cash register. I sold them for five hundred dollars."

"Another small business investment was just as bizarre," confessed Meyer. "I sold a fellow some insurance and took in three dump trucks for the premium. I had *Meyer Top Soil, Sand and Gravel* painted on the trucks and hired three men to run them. I not only didn't know what I was doing, but I was giving no management effort to the business. I kept coming up short every month despite the fact that the men were working hard. I couldn't understand why it wasn't working.

"Friends finally clued me in that the drivers used the trucks at night to take out their girl friends. Also, I would fill the big gas tanks and they would siphon out the gas! Eventually, one night, one of the drivers turned over in one of the trucks. I canceled the insurance and got rid of the trucks and concluded my trucking business," declared Paul. He learned a valuable lesson from this investment: there must be a system to inspect what you expect. You must give attention to the business yourself or hire someone to whom you delegate both the responsibility and the authority to do it for you."

Yet even in adversity, Paul remained self-confident. "If a person has a goal and a belief in it and is enthusiastic and works, the pay-off is going to come like bananas in bunches—or like the Bible promise—'packed down, pressed together, and running over,'" he firmly believes.

CREATIVITY IN REACHING GOALS

Soon after his income from selling whole life insurance had begun to be dependable, Paul decided that he wanted to live in the nicest section of town. He began to look around and soon located a lot that particularly appealed to him. It was owned by Mr. W. G. Salter who had traded Paul the dump trucks for the premium on a policy. Paul told him that he wanted the lot but had no money. He offered to sell some lots for Mr. Salter and take the lot he wanted as his commission. Mr. Salter agreed. He was building in another section of town a group of small brick homes, and Paul agreed to sell thirty houses for his lot. The result was that Paul sold all thirty of the houses in thirty days. That took care of the lot he wanted.

Paul was equally inventive in getting the house built. "I hired my young Sunday school teacher to build the house. Neither of us had any money, but I said, 'I'll make enough money every week to meet the Friday payroll.' Of course, that had to be in addition to normal business and living expenses." During the construction period, Paul sold life insurance policies to fifty-two people who worked on the house—subcontractors and crew alike. One day his friend Jim Hendrix came by and found Paul dressed in his best business suit, with his sales kit "sitting like an Indian on the edge of the roof, talking to a guy on a ladder who was busily soldering the gutters." Jim admitted that he had been worried about Paul's ability to pay for the house, but his anxiety was dispelled after he came upon this scene.

Paul wanted to go first class—he wanted to have Youngstown kitchen cabinets; so he traded the owner of the appliance company the premium on a life insurance policy for the cabinets. He also traded premiums for the drapes, the furniture he used in his home office, and a TV set. Paul confesses that he was as good at bartering as he was at selling; one reason he became so adept was "that a deadline presents a sense of urgency."

Paul admits that inside himself is "a big child," and he promised himself rewards for reaching goals. In 1950 when he led his company in sales, he rewarded himself with a new Cadillac, a new suit, new shoes, and a new briefcase. "I thought the world was mine on the downhill pull," he recalls with jocularity. "That morning my first call was to a fellow at the Stewart Electric Company. I parked my car out front, got out, closed the door, and confidently walked in." The prospect said, "Young man, I don't know what you're selling, but I'm going to buy some of it."

From this experience Paul learned that "what people buy from you is the image you have of yourself and that you convey to their subconscious mind." He illustrates this by recounting an experience that brought the truth home to him. "I once saw John Connally, a renowned Texas governor, walk into a room. . . he absolutely captivated everybody in that room." One's physical appearance affects the impression others gain, but it is the underlying attitude of self-confidence that gives life to the outward appearance.

Paul's exploits in bartering would put the American Indian to shame. "One time in Dalton, Georgia, I swapped a side of beef for a policy. That didn't turn out to be too good a deal, though," Paul remembers. "I didn't stop to think I would have to pay to have it cut up and prepared for the freezer—and I didn't have a freezer. I hurriedly purchased a freezer while the meat was being cut. Unfortunately, we went away for a short trip a few days later, and while we were gone, something went wrong with the freezer. When we got home, the meat was spoiled, and the freezer was so permeated with the odor that I had to get rid of it." But he remembers other trades that worked better. "I've even swapped eggs, vegetables, yard work, cleaning for premiums. . . " Then he told the story of trading a policy for a five carat diamond ring. "The policy's annual premium was $2,000 and I was paid a seventy percent commission. Of course I took a lot of kidding from the people in the home office. But they were always eager to see what I'd bring in next."

Paul always found something the prospect could use for a premium. "One time I called on the owner of a Chevrolet dealership in Dothan, Alabama. He tried to put me off by saying he didn't have any money. So I asked, 'If you *had* the money, would you buy?' The answer was affirmative. Then I said, 'Let's find something you do have.' So I swapped a policy for a brand new 1953 Chevrolet convertible. You should have seen the looks on the faces of the people in the office when I brought that thing back; but I sold it for a nice profit." Paul Meyer was learning to be innovative—maybe even invincible!

RECOGNITION

Perhaps excerpts from the company's records are the most convincing proof of Paul Meyer's dedication to purpose. Here are some headlines from the company's house organs:

> Dec. 5, 1950: $51,000 puts Meyer in the *Million Dollar Production Class.*
>
> Dec. 12, 1950: "Paul Meyer leads Sales Force for 1950."

The article below that last headline reads like this:

> When December's final business figures were compiled, we were able to indulge in "I told you so," for way out in front was Paul Meyer, with a gross production of business written

> over one million dollars... This alone would be a feat worthy of our highest praise, but Paul Meyer not only leads the company in personally producing business, but also found time as Regional Manager of Columbus territory to establish and manage an A-1 agency force. His splendid record for 1950 testifies not only to his unusual capabilities but also to his consistent outlay of hard work.

Meyer became a full-time agent for this small company on March 6, 1951; and it was certainly a logical move, for he was the company's top producer every month of 1951. The weekly reports show his continued productivity and on June 8, 1951, Paul's portfolio carried this information:

Paul J. Meyer, State Manager
Member Million Dollar Round Table – 1950–51

Records reveal that he was the youngest agent ever to attain membership in the Million Dollar Round Table. Meyer's success continued to be unchallenged. Then on October 9, 1951, the company produced a special "flier" that paid tribute to their young agent:

> With a fellow like Paul Meyer around, wonders will never cease and miracles will continue to be performed. Paul's accomplishments week before last were incredible in his production of $181,515 of new business. This week he does the impossible by writing applications for $250,000. This *weekly* production equals what is considered average *annual* production for the average agent.

The article also records facts about Paul Meyer's early insurance career, citing his first experience on a debit in 1948 with a small company in Jacksonville, Florida.

> But Paul Meyer promptly broke all production records in that company's history. By 1950, associated with a relatively small company,... he made personal sales amounting to $1,165,000 face amount in two months. In 1951 his face value volume reached $3,812,000 [all in 20-pay life policies]. For three straight years he led the company and was made Vice President and Superintendent of Agencies.

The company was proud of Paul Meyer. The Controller General and Insurance Commissioner of Georgia, Zack D. Cravey, wrote Meyer a letter on November 28, 1951:

> McCart told me of the marvelous sales record you have made since April 3, 1950—applications for nearly $2,750,000 this year is almost unbelievable, as was your total last year. . . I know too of the active interest you are taking in religious and civic affairs. Good citizens can perform no nobler services. . .

Another letter Paul received is worthy of transcription—a note from the company President, Harold McCart, on December 26, 1951:

> Your records since you started with us in March, 1950, are on my desk, and I find it almost impossible to believe the facts disclosed by an examination of the records. If anyone anywhere since the beginning of the life insurance business has ever equaled your production record with us, I have never heard about it. I am confident that I will not be challenged by making the statement that your accomplishments have never been equaled.

A confirmation of this statement came in a letter dated August 15, 1958, from Hal C. Nutt, Purdue University, Life Insurance Marketing Institute, Layfayette, Indiana:

> To my knowledge, your record of production during your early years in the life insurance business has never been excelled by any other new salesman in the long history of our present agency system.

Some of the figures quoted as records set by Paul in insurance sales sound small by comparison with productivity for insurance people today. It must be remembered, however, that the insurance business has undergone a great deal of change in thirty years. All of the insurance records Paul set were in twenty-year pay life and endowment policies that averaged from thirty dollars a thousand up to one thousand dollars a thousand in annual premiums. When the effect of inflation over the last thirty odd years is considered, these figures are phenomenal. They represent as much as or more than the actual production of the top insurance salespeople in the industry today.

Previously Paul had found time to become a graduate of Purdue's Life Insurance Marketing Institute, and with this credible insurance training behind him, Paul, in April, 1953, joined the largest exclusive ordinary life insurance company in the nation. This move was made as a result of what he considered a lack of reward for his achievements.

Young Paul believed in the credo—"the more you grow, the more your opportunities grow." With his incredible record, he wanted more than money—he wanted advancement. He wanted to be made a vice-president of the company, a position he had earlier earned with the first company for which he had sold ordinary or whole life insurance. But this company refused. "You're too young yet. . . you should be at least twenty-six," he was told. Paul was only twenty-three! He believed that rewards should be given for achievement—not age. He couldn't wait. He sent in his resignation.

About that time, he chanced to be in Coral Gables on vacation and passed an office of one of the companies that had been actively recruiting him for three years. "I retraced my steps, walked through the door and asked to see the General Agent. I was attracted to this particular agency because I knew the general Agent, Virgil Wright, was the leader in the company. I walked in and told him I had talked to Charlie Becker in the home office, and just wondered if Charlie was still interested in having me in the company. Mr. Wright called Becker on the phone, and I asked him what he would do for me if I joined the company and became #1 in sales. He promised me a trip around the world. This was during the Christmas holidays in 1952. In January 1953 I moved to the company." The company journal of July 1953 carried a picture and story on their new agent:

> A good-looking twenty-four-year-old boy said to me recently, "I have always shot for a star, as I have found out that is the best way to reach the mountain. You can have anything you want in life if you crystallize your thinking as to what you want,. . . you must have a plan," said the new associate in the Airline Division of Florida.

In his first sixty days, Paul completed 150 sales for a volume of over $1,000,000 and subsequently qualified for the Million Dollar Round Table in 1952, as he had in 1950 and 1951. The company's July journal printed a *salute* to their new agent—Paul J. Meyer. The author of the story wanted to know "What makes this boy tick?" At the end of an evening with Paul Meyer he reached this conclusion:

> He has a highly developed competitive spirit. There is in him an insatiable yearning, not just to be good, not just to be better than most, but to be the best. His spirit brooks no peers. Competition is simply a goal to greater effort, as it is to a spirited race horse.

As proof of this analysis, in June Paul Meyer was named "Man of the Month" by the company as a result of sales in excess of $400,000.

Paul Meyer learned much from his early insurance career. One great personal victory for the young man is indicative of his courage and determination. Either from impatience with himself or an actual physical circumstance, young Meyer suffered from a slight speech hesitation—almost a stutter. He thought faster than he could verbalize! He conquered the problem by following a personally disciplined program—reading aloud for thirty minutes a day for *four* years. In addition he invested about $12,000 in speech therapy at the University of Miami and accepted every opportunity to speak in public until he mastered the problem and became an excellent platform performer as well as a persuasive salesperson in an individual presentation. He now modestly makes light of that monumental achievement. He often tells salespeople that weaknesses must be turned into strengths; to illustrate this principle, he tells how he persisted in making sales presentations in spite of his speech hesitation, humorously claiming that prospects often signed the application just from compassion—to put an end to his suffering, or to save themselves from witnessing any more of his struggles.

This victory through persistence brought with it an additional bonus. Paul learned to read widely, yet critically, thus enriching his life with a continually increasing wealth of knowledge and interests. And he reaffirmed his faith in the axiom, "It's not what happens to you, but what you do about it that matters."

Obstacles in the way of needed skills and personality traits and environmental conditions never posed a problem for Paul Meyer. He just did what was necessary to develop skills and personality traits or to change conditions. What was harder for him to surmount was criticism that seemed rooted largely in jealousy. As his success began to bring him recognition and praise from the company officers, he frequently encountered hostility from others who somehow felt threatened by his outstanding personal productivity. Some of his colleagues complained that he was motivated by the desire to make them look bad by comparison. Those who had previously been recognized as top producers resented having to take second place to this *young upstart*. Such criticism hurt Paul—much as he had been hurt by what he had, in childhood, interpreted as his father's lack of approval. But with characteristic individualism, Paul refused to allow criticism or opposition to divert him from his chosen goals. These experiences led to the addition of point five to his *Million Dollar Personal Success Plan:*

> Develop a dogged determination to follow through on your plan regardless of obstacles, criticism or circumstances or what other people say, think or do.

The *Million Dollar Personal Success Plan* became Paul Meyer's written strategy for achievement. Its name came from his goal to become a millionaire through insurance selling—a goal he reached at the age of twenty-seven—by consistently following that plan.

Paul sold insurance with determination, for he believed in it, and he became personally involved with his clients. He wanted what would be best for them, as well as the sale of the policies. In his orderly files he has preserved every sales kit he ever used, as well as lists of all of his policy holders. The entire business was personal to him, and he remembers the people and the circumstances, even today.

CHAPTER THREE

GAINING MATURITY

You create your own environment — mental, emotional and physical — by the attitudes you develop.

Paul J. Meyer

CHAPTER THREE

GAINING MATURITY

EXPANDING INTERESTS

Some time after Paul Meyer moved to South Florida and continued his insurance selling activity in the Miami area, he met Dr. William (Bill) Hinson, his pastor at the Wayside Baptist Church of Kendall, Florida. They quickly became close personal friends in addition to their more formal relationship, and Dr. Hinson became a valued confidant for the young Meyer who savored the success and recognition he was receiving but was determined that they be earned in the context of his own high values and ethical standards.

Dr. Hinson's memories of the Paul Meyer of the mid 1950's include observing Paul's excitement in growing success, the flamboyance of the young entrepreneur reveling in the rewards of achievement, and the yearning of the youthful businessman to make certain that his success was meaningful—that it contributed something worthwhile to the lives of others as well as producing financial rewards for himself. Dr. Hinson has continued to maintain a close relationship to Paul over the years. He has seen Paul's growth to maturity, not only in the area of business success, but in the clarification of personal values that serve as a direction for his life.

In spite of his colorful life style at this period, young Paul Meyer was always conscious of others and their needs. He constantly sought to help others experience the same joy in success that he had and to make full use of their potential for achievement. When he first started managing salespeople, he began to give them books and articles to read on various personal development topics. Later, he would ask what they thought about those items. Far too often for Paul to understand, it turned out that they had not read what he had given them.

Eventually, he formed the habit of spending at least ten or fifteen minutes of each early-morning sales meeting reading to his salespeople from some book or article that he knew could help them build more positive attitudes, identify their own goals, or strengthen their sales skills.

But his interest in helping salespeople did not stop with those who were members of his own organization. Once a Fuller Brush salesman approached his house. From his living room window, Paul saw a bushy-haired man drive up to the house, start to park in the driveway, then back up, hesitate in front of the house, and finally move on to park in front of the vacant lot next door. Paul watched him get out of the car and walk back to the house.

With a characteristic mixture of concern for the individual and playful mischief, Paul developed an immediate plan of action. When the salesman knocked on the door, Paul was ready for him. He jerked the door open at the first rap and asked, "Are you trying to sell me something?" The poor, unsuspecting salesman was aghast. He stammered. Paul pressed on, "Is that your car over there?" When the salesman admitted it was, Paul demanded, "Go get it. We have to rebuild your approach." Too shocked to protest, the confused man drove the car into the driveway, and Paul asked, "Have you ever been in a Rolls Royce?" The answer was a timid negative.

"Let me show you how you would get out of a Rolls Royce." Paul sat behind the wheel, then stepped out, closed the door carefully, brushed an imaginary speck of dust off the rear-view mirror, took a step or two, then turned around and looked back at the car with pride. Then he walked purposefully up to the house and firmly and confidently knocked on the door. "Now," Paul said, "I'm going back into the house; then I want you to knock again as if you had just climbed out of a Rolls Royce." The man executed the procedure until Paul was satisfied that he understood what was needed. Paul's next step was to take the brush salesman to a clothing store and photograph him in a handsome new suit, then to a car agency for a polaroid shot standing next to a smart new car. "Look at these pictures every day," Paul instructed the salesman, "and believe that this is the *real you. Feel* successful! *Act* successful! Then you will *be* successful."

Five years later, the same Fuller Brush salesman again knocked on Paul's front door. But he looked and acted like a different person. He told Paul of his activities during the intervening years. He had progressed from last place to first as a representative for Fuller Brush in the state of Florida and had become regional manager. He hugged Paul and expressed his gratitude for that push in the right direction. Paul gives full credit for this success to the salesman himself who took the ideas given to him and used them to achieve his own goals. But it was Paul Meyer who had provided the inspiration and the initial belief that helped this one among many to find the key to success.

ENJOYING LIFE'S ABUNDANCE

While he helped others, he also indulged his own desires—and used his own advice to look, feel, and act out his personal anticipation of success. Paul Meyer remembers an example of that attitude of anticipation, in the early 1950's. He had decided to go for a bit of rest to Daytona Beach because the vice-president of the insurance company recommended that city as a good vacation spot. He stayed a week and the hotel bill was $350. "I was about twenty-one at the time, and I didn't carry around that kind of money. So I called our general agent in Daytona Beach, Biff Carr, a genial man about sixty, and told him of my situation. He wanted to loan me $350."

But Paul refused. "Biff," Paul declared, "I didn't call you to bail me out. You must have a prospect you haven't sold. What commission do you work on?" The answer was "seventy percent." Paul asked Biff to pick him up at the hotel. "I told him," Paul relates, "that we'd go to see his toughest prospect or one he hadn't been able to sell. Then I promised him that I would sell that prospect a policy with a minimum premium of $1,000 and we would split the seven hundred dollar, or larger, commission—or Biff could turn in the business and pay my hotel bill. So we went to see a man who owned an ice plant on Highway One and had two children. We sold him a policy with a $500 premium for each child, bringing in the $1,000 premium and a seven hundred dollar commission. Biff paid my hotel bill and I went home." Paul's confidence knew no bounds. He was willing to take risks because he believed in his ability to meet any challenge. He attracted associates and friends who shared his courage and daring, and his enjoyment of a fast-paced life style.

The young human dynamo saw the world as a source of great abundance, and he believed in earning his share of a rich life. But he never thought that it was necessary to win his own riches at the expense of others. He believed that all people could share in the good life if they

Confidence in yourself gives you a clear vision of your goal and creates desire that is strong enough to sweep away all obstacles.

Paul J. Meyer

had faith in themselves and their abilities. Consequently, he believed that all people deserve a chance to prove themselves—a chance to succeed. For Paul, prejudice was always merely a word in the dictionary—never an attitude.

SHARING LIFE'S ABUNDANCE

One day Meyer was driving from Valdosta to Tifton, Georgia, in a hard rain. Blinded by the downpour, he spun off the road into a ditch. He climbed out of the ditch and up an embankment to an old, unpainted farm house about fifty feet away. A black man met him at the door. When Paul explained his problem, the man cranked up his tractor and pulled the car out of the ditch. But the rain was still so heavy that Paul gladly accepted an invitation to stay until the weather improved. The new acquaintances talked; and before the rain had stopped, Paul had recruited his new friend into the insurance business. The man became highly successful. In his first year he sold over two million dollars face value in permanent life insurance—an almost unprecedented feat at that time. This personal production put him in the top one percent of all insurance salespeople in the nation. He eventually sold practically all of the black teachers in the state of Florida, made enough money to buy a bigger farm, and experienced a complete turn-around in his life. "And I met him in a ditch!" Paul exclaimed. "He was warm, articulate, charming—and a very sharp guy," Paul concluded, emanating a sense of joy as he recalled the excitement of seeing the success this man was able to achieve.

Such incidents are numerous in the life of Paul Meyer, for *people* are his hobby. Paul's friend and co-worker Bill Armor recalls picking up Larry Leavitt as a hitch-hiker on a Florida highway. Leavitt was from New Jersey, slovenly dressed and unshaven, and had just been through a divorce. Bill brought him to Paul because Paul had always said, "We don't judge people; we give them an opportunity to prove themselves." So the pair cleaned Leavitt up and took him to Armor's agency where a seventy-seven-day sales contest was in progress. Larry Leavitt won first place in the contest! "Someone had faith in me," he declared.

Another incident is indicative of Paul's belief in the potential of the individual. Paul once called at a home in Miami to sell some insurance to a prospect named Dugan. He learned that Mr. Dugan had recently been injured in an automobile accident; so Paul recruited his wife, Mrs. Polly Dugan, to sell insurance. She proved highly productive, attaining membership in the Million Dollar Round Table. Later she won recognition as a top producer in the company. She became a millionaire, for she invested her earnings in pre-built condominiums on the Florida coast.

The length of Paul Meyer's "friendship list" is staggering. It embraces all ages, colors, and creeds. To untold people he has been the man by the side of the road who extended a helping hand—not as charity, but as a demonstration of the kind of faith in another's potential that provides a much-needed boost to self-confidence.

THE MILLION DOLLAR GOALS

When he first began selling insurance, Paul's goal had been to sell a million dollars worth of insurance in a year—then a million in a month—then a million in a week—and finally a million in a day! When he had achieved the first three of these goals, it became evident that the latter goal could not be easily accomplished through individual, one-on-one selling. The day he set out to reach his goal of a million in a day is a memorable one for him—not only because of his success in reaching that goal, but because it taught him the powerful principle of group selling that he has passed on to his sales organization.

It was on January 26, 1955, at the McAlister Hotel in Miami that the stage was set for realization of the goal. Paul had planned his sales strategy carefully. He had printed out a prospectus on the insurance policy and handed out copies to his audience. Then he told them that they were going to catch a glimpse of the life and operation of an entrepreneur. "I had a medical examiner set up a little booth. I had my policy painted on a 4 × 8 foot flip-chart. As I talked, I'd turn those sheets. That day I sold $1,250,000 in life insurance. As people signed applications, I sent them through the medical examining booth and collected the premium." How did he get the prospects there? He had invited them to lunch!

There is also an aftermath to the McAlister story. A young man in Yankton, South Dakota, heard the story and invited fifteen hundred people to breakfast in a gymnasium in Yankton. He sold 277 policies and set the record for his company. Subsequently he and Paul became friends by mail.

MULTIPLE SALES

Along with sales to large groups of people, Paul developed additional income from selling to a number of individuals who worked for one company. One such venture came as the result of a lead from a friend. Charlie Skinner told Paul of a large bakery in Tallahassee whose owner would be a fine insurance prospect. Paul hopped on an Eastern Airlines plane and flew to Tallahassee, took a motel room, then went with Charlie to call on the baker. He was a tall Texan who said, "I don't have time to talk to you—I'm going to Pensacola."

Paul was not upset. "I reached out my hand and said, 'Meet your chauffeur,' I didn't want to lose my prospect now. If he was leaving town, I was leaving with him. So all the way to Pensacola I questioned him about his life story. He told me how he had started the company, where he got the money—I got a whole course in management on that ride—it was wonderful! When we got to Pensacola he asked me what I wanted. I told him that I just wanted to make a salary savings program available to his employees. 'It won't cost you anything. It can be done by a payroll deduction.' I showed him the policy—he liked me—and the plan.

"Back at the office he gave me a desk and told the manager to run in the employees one at a time. There were about sixty employees at the plant, and I sold them all on the plan. Then I realized that the bakery was open all night. So I worked all night and got the rest of them. The next morning I was still going strong when a repairman came in to fix an air-conditioning duct. He was listening to me—so I sold him, too; I didn't want to miss anybody." Paul Meyer sold 106 people on this excursion and was back home in forty-eight hours. Needless to say, that month he led the whole company. And in appreciation for the lead, Paul gave Charlie Skinner his fishing boat!

A SPECIAL INSURANCE FRIEND

The insurance business welded friendships for Paul Meyer. One such friend was Bill Armor. "Bill Armor was quite a salesman—we used to call him Mr. Enthusiasm," Paul commented. "Once we were in Birmingham, Alabama, to call on a prospect. Bill picked up the three-ring binder that he used as a visual aid in his sales pitch. We were greeted by the prospect. Then Bill began. 'Mr. Jones, let me show you something—you haven't ever seen anything like it! It's absolutely phenomenal! Mind if I push this back?' and he pushed aside some papers on the desk and moved his chair closer. In almost a whisper, he said, 'I want you to see this!' (Those vocal variations always shook me up; yet I had to keep a straight face to remain professional.) Then in his awe-inspiring ritual he gave the opening of the sales presentation, jumped to the close, and then got the signed application and the check for $1,000."

The two were almost to the car when Paul exploded, "Armor, did anyone ever tell you that you don't know what you're talking about?"

"What do you mean, I don't know what I'm talking about?" Bill bristled. "I got the sale!"

"Unless my memory fails me, you missed two-thirds of that presentation. Remember, I wrote it! You just passed over the middle as if it weren't even there!" And it wasn't!

"By then we had reached the car and in the back seat were pages 11 thru 50 of the sales kit. We laughed our heads off," recalled Paul. "That's the greatest proof in the world that if you have a good opening and a good close, most of the conversation in between must be designed just to entertain the salesperson, not to inform the prospect."

Paul Meyer loves to run through his repertoire of stories about Bill Armor. Once when he was Bill's sales manager in Miami, Paul received a call from a man unknown to him. "I'm not mad, and this is not a complaint. I just want to talk to somebody." The caller seemed uncertain how to proceed. "Don't hang up on me. I just want to ask a question," the gentle voice continued. So Meyer took his name, address, and phone number. Then the caller became even more hesitant, but finally revealed his concern. "A young man," he said, "came in here and sold me a life insurance policy and I gave him nine hundred dollars. I wonder if somebody will explain to me what I bought."

Meyer was dismayed—and amused. "Why," he asked, "would you give somebody nine hundred dollars if you didn't understand it? Why didn't you ask *him* about it?"

The genteel voice answered, "Oh, you didn't see him come into my store. He was the most enthusiastic young man I have ever seen in my life."

Then things "clicked" for Paul Meyer. "Was his name Bill Armor?"

"Yes, yes, that's it!" came the expected reply. And it's easy to see why Bill's friends nicknamed him "Mr. Enthusiasm." He's convincing!

Bill Armor exhibited some of the flamboyance that characterized Paul Meyer also at this period. Once on a golf course in Ft. Lauderdale—most likely after he had made an especially good drive—Bill bragged that he could walk into someone's office in his golf shoes and hat and with his golf bag over his shoulder and sell him a life insurance policy. Paul challenged him, "How much do you want to bet?"

"We finished the game," Paul tells, "then from the phone book we picked out a name—a dentist, Dr. Roger Stockman. And we were on our way." Bill, in his golf attire, approached the receptionist. "I've got to see the doctor—quick!" Paul could hardly keep his face straight, but Bill was escorted to the doctor, whom he told, "This is a matter of life or death!"—which, of course, it was—life or death for his bet! The doctor dismissed the patient in his chair—only to find himself listening to Bill's sales pitch. When he realized what had happened, everyone laughed."

Dr. Stockman liked Armor instantly and Bill sold him a life insurance policy. Subsequently, the pair became fast friends, and the doctor still enjoys telling friends the story of his "life or death" dentistry. Stockman and Armor continued their friendship over the years, making annual hunting and fishing trips together; and Stockman remained a good client for Armor, buying insurance from him repeatedly. And Paul continues to call Bill "Mr. Enthusiasm."

A SPECIAL FRIENDSHIP

Some of Paul Meyer's best friends came from experiences just as unusual as that of Dr. Stockman and Bill Armor. For Paul, getting the sale and reaching the goal have always been serious, but having fun along the way and enjoying the thrill of the chase continue to be important aspects of his enjoyment of success. Was it Bill Armor whose *joie de vivre* rubbed off on Paul Meyer—or *vice versa?* The story of Paul's introduction to W. Clement Stone is a close rival to the Armor/Stockman tale.

Paul had long wanted to meet W. Clement Stone, head of the Combined Insurance Company of America, at that time the largest exclu-

sive accident insurance company in the world, based in Chicago. Once Paul heard that Mr. Stone was staying at the Fontainbleu Hotel where he was to fill a speaking engagement. Paul immediately decided that this was a once-in-a-lifetime opportunity to fulfill his goal of meeting the man he considered an inspiration and a role model. He walked confidently through the lobby, proceeded to the elevator, then to Mr. Stone's suite; but he was not allowed to enter. After a bit of fast thinking, Meyer went back downstairs, "borrowed" a waiter's napkin and a tray, returned upstairs and again knocked on the door. "Mr. Stone himself opened the door and I entered," recalled Meyer with a sly grin. "Then I started laughing and confessed my ruse. . . and we've been friends ever since."

As unlikely as the story seems, it is typical of the inventiveness, the courage, and the self-assurance of one who believes in himself. Paul reasons, of course, "If you don't have faith in yourself, how can you expect anyone else to believe in you?" Subsequently, W. Clement Stone was one of the people who supported Meyer in the early days of building his dream—Success Motivation Institute.

When the fledgling company was about two years old, it had—like many successful young companies—grown so rapidly that it had outstripped Meyer's ability to provide adequate capital. When Meyer sought expansion financing in Waco, no one was willing to back him. He called Mr. Stone and told him of the problem. Mr. Stone told Paul to come to Chicago, bring a copy of his goals for the company and his plan of action for achieving them. Paul did, and Mr. Stone was impressed with the plan. He confided that he had never before seen such a clear, concise yet complete plan of action or goals program for any business. Stone immediately took Paul to the American National Bank in Chicago and endorsed Paul's note for $200,000 in return for ten per cent of the dream. True to his plan, Paul paid off the note in two years and later bought back Stone's shares in the company, giving Stone a handsome profit.

RECOGNITION AS A CHAMPION

Paul Meyer's voluminous letter files reveal an almost day-by-day record of his life. Excerpts from a number of letters found in those files of 1957–1959 are of particular significance in his life insurance sales career, for they came from figures of eminence in the American insurance field, as well as from other prominent successful people.

AL WATSON—April 11, 1957, Macon, Georgia

Today I received something in the mail for which I think you deserve the real credit. On January 11, 1956 I went to work for the N.Y.L.I. Co., and in my first year with them I became a member of the Million Dollar Round Table. The plaque came just a few minutes ago.

As I look back over the past year. . . I find that I was doing exactly the things you taught me to do while I was in college. . . You instilled in me the determination, confidence, and the work habits that brought me to my recently attained Million Dollar Round Table.

BILL ARMOR—Aug. 6, 1958, Great Plains, Wyoming Life Insurance Company

Through your association, enthusiasm, and motivation I acquired the necessary ability to start the company I head today. Throughout the years I have employed your sales and motivation techniques not only in the production of new business, but in the handling of men. Your methods have proved highly successful and most pertinent to building a strong and aggressive sales organization.

HAROLD LANIGAN, May 24, 1959, Miami, Florida, Florida State Manager for All America Life & Casualty Co. Chicago, Illinois

You will recall that during my first year in the insurance business that I never missed one of your meetings. That was because I was convinced that a year of creative sales ideas, if put into practice, meant the stepping stones to success. You will be happy to know that my company has just presented me with the highest award afforded a member of our Field force for 1958. . . Since you were such a motivating influence. . . your inspiration and assistance always come to my mind whenever I receive recognition.

Your sincere belief and conviction that the young men in America can still accomplish anything for which they are willing to pay the price and your unending enthusiasm and positive outlook on life, have possibly been the strongest influence toward what success I have achieved.

CLAUDE PEPPER, May 6, 1959, Law Offices—Miami, Florida, —(also United States Senator from Florida)

—congratulations on *Success Story* as one of leading salesmen in America—known to us prior to meeting you in 1955. . . . also we know of the grueling experience you had with National Union Life and it was evident to us, as it was to all of us who were familiar with the situation that your great personal effort and sacrifice were an inspiration to others in the company and played an important part in the rehabilitation of the company.

It is refreshing to note that you are not bitter about your experience with National Union, but have taken the attitude that it was educational and that the lessons you learned are now an asset to you.

Your ability to inspire, motivate and wake up *the sleeping giant* in others is your greatest asset.

WAYNE PHILPOTT, June 27, 1959, Audio Record Library Company, Dallas, Texas

Never has a man looked so deeply into my being and awakened the determination and enthusiasm for successful living as you have, Paul. And my wife says: "I enjoy living with the revised version!"

DR. RUSSELL A. WILLIAMS, June 27, 1959, Vice-President, Biscayne Federal Savings & Loan Association

. . .[your] leadership, optimistic outlook on life, need of a definite purpose in all undertakings—all qualities nourished with kindliness and faith and intellectual honesty have brought their certain reward.

KNOX WYATT, June 23, 1953, C.L.U. State Manager, Rome, Georgia, Franklin Life Insurance Company

—congratulations on continued leadership in Ranking Number One Man among all [company] representatives. *You are doing the very thing you said you would do if you ever joined us.*

CHARLIE SALLASKA, July 13, 1959, Sallaska Enterprises, Inc. Warsaw, Indiana

> —[I] first met Paul on Aug. 15, St. Louis, Missouri, when he handed out the Million Dollar Plan. Then I read: "You can have anything you want in life if you follow through on the Success Plan."
>
> One other thing you said to me last year I have never forgotten: "Charlie, remember you are where you are and what you are financially—and spiritually because of the dominating thoughts that occupy your mind." I literally brainwash myself every day with that idea.

Paul's continued success seemed assured. He had proved that he could overcome personal obstacles, develop new skills, manage a sales force—anything that his career demanded. He could not imagine encountering a major setback that would wipe out everything he had worked so hard to achieve.

CHAPTER FOUR
WINDS OF CHANGE

In every adversity
is the seed of an
equivalent –
or greater –
benefit.

Paul J. Meyer

CHAPTER FOUR

WINDS OF CHANGE

WHEN SETBACK OCCURS

Paul Meyer's phenomenal success in life insurance sales brought him attention from many people in the business community. He was always eager to meet other successful business people with whom he could share ideas and from whom he could learn. One person he met during this time was a man who had established a new insurance company and was looking for "the right person" to head up sales. As an inducement to join the company, he promised Paul exclusive marketing rights and an option to purchase ten percent of the company. Paul was enough of an entrepreneur to listen. Here was his chance to run the sales division for an entire company. He accepted the offer and signed the contract. "Thereafter, we were partners. Every time I made a dollar, he got half of it," recalled Meyer. I recruited eight hundred thirty-two people in one year, and we soon sold so much insurance that we outsold the company's surplus.

In retrospect, Paul realizes that now he would know that a surplus the size that company possessed is too small to support the type of expansion represented by the sales volume he created. But his youthful lack of experience, his excitement at being in full charge of sales, his enjoyment of financial success, and the heady intoxication of being at the center of a whirlwind operation pushed him ahead. To add to the company's shaky financial condition resulting from such large sales in a short time, Paul's partner was quietly siphoning funds from the company. This was a circumstance Paul never dreamed could occur. His almost naive trust and belief in the innate goodness of others blinded him to the possibility that someone he loved as a friend and trusted as a business associate could betray him.

Then the incredible happened! One Monday morning Meyer went to the office, took out his key and opened the door. The large building was *empty*. Over the week-end eight vans had moved everything to Alabama! Not a desk, not a single file cabinet remained! "I was in a state of shock," Paul recalls, "but when I collected my senses, I called a good friend who was a member of the company's Board of Directors. He was astounded. He knew nothing about what had occurred. I eventually learned that the Insurance Commissioner of Florida had asked the company to put up additional assets to cover the surplus shortage. Because the company was domiciled in Alabama, my partner had simply loaded up all the Florida assets and equipment and moved everything back to Alabama. About a million dollars worth of assets were moved out of Florida—everything from the vault and all the records from the bank."

The sequel is sad. Several of the officers were indicted on more than fifty counts; there was at least one suicide, and several deaths among the Directors of the company within twelve months, with stress as a probable contributing cause in most instances.

BOUNCING BACK FROM REVERSES

Meyer was in no way involved in the company policy or financial activities. He was not an officer of the company; he was not a director; he just sold insurance. Not only had Paul now lost his income of about $20,000 a month, but he also felt an overpowering responsibility for the people he had recruited to join the company. He went for advice to an attorney—Claude Pepper, then a U.S. Senator from Florida. He introduced Meyer to Alan Clements, a sharp young attorney in his firm who was about Paul's age. Together they looked over all the options, then told Meyer, "You can simply walk away. It isn't your problem."

But Paul Meyer said, "I feel that it is partly my problem because the people I hired and trained sold all that insurance. What will happen if I stay and help straighten it out?"

Clements explained, "Well, you'll probably be broke. It will take a lot of time and all your money, and in the end you will receive no thanks."

Paul thought only a minute; he had a million dollars worth of personal assets—first mortgages, buildings, AT&T bonds—all very liquid.

So his decision was quick. "I'll stay." Good friend Bill Armor stayed, too, and together they worked for eighteen months without compensation. Meyer sold everything he had and paid the company's liabilities. Then he and Armor found jobs for all the sales force for whom they felt such responsibility. In the course of settling the company's affairs, he went to Dallas to see Theo Beasley, President of Republic National Life Insurance Company, the re-insurance company that had served the Florida operation, and delivered to him $280,000 in premiums that Republic National Life had already written off as uncollectable. The Republic National Life executives were shocked when they were told what Meyer was doing.

In an effort to salvage the company's Florida operation, Republic National Life contacted Mr. McKnight, owner of Minnesota Mining and Manufacturing Company, and negotiated a sale of the operation. Mr. McKnight put up $600,000 worth of 3M stock as collateral to guarantee the surplus shortage and, at the same time, took control of the company.

THE AFTERMATH

When the legal tangle was all cleared out, Paul stood on the steps of the court house, contemplating the contrast between his financial situation now and just a short two years before. At 27 he had been a millionaire. At 29 he was worse than bankrupt—$89,000 in debt. As he stood there, Claude Pepper walked up behind him, put his arm across Meyer's shoulder, and said, "You are the richest young man I have ever met. You could have walked away from this mess and kept your personal fortune intact. You may not have any money left, but you have something of far greater worth—integrity."

For a long time after this experience, Paul Meyer carried in his billfold this quotation from Shakespeare's *Othello:*

> Who steals my purse steals trash. . .
> But he that filches from me my good name
> Robs me of that which not enriches him,
> And makes me poor indeed.

"Hal Roberts, a good friend and pilot who had sold insurance for me, drove me home from the court house in his Cadillac convertible,"

Real confidence
in yourself
is always
demonstrated by
Action!

Paul J. Meyer

Paul remembers. "We sat there in front of my house, and I said, 'Hal, I've got to sell the house—I can't make the next payment on it. Frankly, it's a good thing anyway, because all I ever got out of the insurance business was money. What I enjoyed was working with the sales force and helping motivate them.'" Ideas were beginning to crystalize in Paul Meyer's mind. He was evaluating his life and looking for the best way to reach his dreams. Hal took off a ring that he always wore and showed Paul an inscription inside: "This, too, shall pass." It was a message of hope that Paul believed and held to in the days that followed.

"My neighbor from across the street, Glen McNew, saw me start into the house," Paul said, "and called me over to talk with him. He took me down to the drug store, and we sat together at the soda fountain. Underneath the counter he handed me twenty-five one hundred dollar bills, saying, 'You're a hard person to help. We all get down. This will help you out.' We sat together in that drug store trying to control our tears—his of compassion, and mine of gratitude for such friendship. I took that twenty-five hundred dollars, bought a ticket to Dallas, and went to see Theo Beasley in Dallas at the Republic National Life Insurance Company. He had told me to come to see him if I ever needed help. I told him I wanted to borrow fifty thousand dollars. He immediately said I had the loan—not even asking what I intended to do with it. I took the check and asked what kind of note he wanted me to sign. He just shrugged his shoulders and said, 'None.' I paid it back in about three years."

THE BENEFITS OF ADVERSITY

From all the experiences connected with the failure of the insurance company, Paul learned first-hand the truth he had heard so often from his mother: "Every adversity holds the seed of an equivalent or greater benefit if you believe it, look for it, and work for it."

SEEKING A NEW DIRECTION

Offers began to pour in from insurance companies promising lucrative contracts and sales deals. Paul's demonstrated personal expertise in selling, his experience in recruiting and training an effective sales or-

A common reason
for human failure
is total disregard
for the power
of self-motivation.

Paul J. Meyer

ganization, and his obvious personal integrity were paying off. "I was reluctant to move in that direction," Paul recalls, " to the mystification of all my friends. I didn't think I'd ever sell life insurance again," Paul reminisced. "But I changed my mind. I made plans to build an insurance company from scratch. After all, I'd had experience. Soon, I had raised half a million dollars and named the Board of Directors for the proposed Eastern States Life Insurance Company."

When he applied for a Florida charter, Paul and Bill Armor were invited to a hotel room in Daytona Beach, only to discover that there was to be a $25,000 under-the-table payoff, ostensibly to hire an attorney as a consultant. Meyer's answer was "If I have to start a company by cheating, God knows where I'll end! You have just closed a chapter in my life." That half a million dollars Paul had raised was returned to the investors.

THE BIRTH OF AN IDEA

At this critical time, Paul Meyer remained in close contact with his pastor, Dr. Bill Hinson, who later became pastor of the First Baptist Church in New Orleans, and is now with Baylor University in Waco, Texas. Dr. Hinson has subsequently had a great influence on Meyer's life. During these days of disappointment Dr. Hinson met frequently with Paul, served as a willing listener, and encouraged him as he sought new direction for his life and career.

One evening as sunset gave way to evening, Paul Meyer walked on the beach with Bill Hinson. To his pastor, Paul confided his determination to find a new career. He was through selling life insurance. He still believed in life insurance, and he was grateful for what it had given him in his life. But he confided to Bill that what he enjoyed most about selling life insurance was the opportunity to interact with salespeople and clients, talking about motivation and setting and achieving goals. He had learned a great deal about these subjects, but he didn't see how this knowledge and experience could be used as a career.

At one point in the conversation, Bill Hinson remarked, "Paul, it appears to me that you are happiest when you are helping people to see how they can reach their own goals and be successful. Why don't you start a company with that as its purpose?"

The simple question struck a responsive chord in Paul. This concise expression of all his desires and dreams seemed to act as a catalyst to bring together all the plans and ideas that had been churning in his mind. He told Bill, however, that he saw one very big obstacle: "I have no education in or information about the communication industry."

Bill had an immediate suggestion. "I just happen to know someone you ought to meet," he told Paul. "Jarrell McCracken, about ten years ago, started a company in Waco, Texas, called Word, Inc., that publishes and markets religious recordings. They are beginning to make a real impact in the industry."

Bill Hinson arranged the meeting of the two men. It was now early 1957. McCracken traveled to Miami to see Meyer and visited him at his home. When he saw that impressive house, McCracken said with a laugh, "You make more than our whole company takes in!" Paul's response was, "If I decide to join your company, you won't have to pay me anything except a commission on what I sell. I'll start at the bottom."

MARKING TIME

In the ninety-day period before Paul and Word finalized their agreement, Paul found an opportunity to learn something about franchising. A company in Minneapolis ran an advertisement in Florida papers for a soft drink franchise. "I investigated," said Paul, always alert to possibilities. "They had a grape mix by Welch, an orange mix by Minute Maid, and chocolate by Carnation. They used a cold drink dispenser with a special valve at the bottom connected to a blender that whipped the drink as it dispensed. The drink was frothy—foamy, really delicious. I was interested in buying the machines as an investment—four hundred dollars down on four hundred machines. Then the owner asked me if I would help him sell them. As I hesitated, considering my desire to learn the franchise business, he said, 'Go test this thing—check it out.' The machine had a copper colored finish; it was perched on a stand of stiff cardboard and had a sewing machine motor to turn the blender. When you pulled down the lever, it would froth the chocolate drink—delicious. So I agreed to test it.

"I took my brother with me. We went to a cafeteria on Wilshire Boulevard in Los Angeles and set up the machine. As people came down the line, they pulled the lever and got the chocolate—with a slip of paper reading, 'If you feel like saying it tastes like Grandma used to make. . .' and a request for a testimonial. Well, one day a heavy-weight pulled the handle and got that blender stuck while it was going full force. The front came off the machine, and chocolate drink spewed on everybody within fifty feet! People reacted in so many different ways that I was tickled. The more everyone scurried around, the funnier the scene became. The manager was angry, my brother was angry, and the chocolate company had to clean everyone's clothes. Needless to say, no one else appreciated my laughter."

Paul Meyer continually ran into interesting situations—and people. One day in Minneapolis, when the temperature was about 10° below zero, he was walking down the street with his chocolate machine under his arm. He caught up with an elderly man who was hunched against the cold wind. Characteristically, Paul started a conversation. The older man had lived in Minneapolis all his life and was planning a Florida retirement, while Paul had come to Minnesota from Florida. Aghast that anyone would *choose* to come to that frigid climate, the man exclaimed, "Young man! Go back! Go Back!" He thought Paul was out of his mind to leave sunny Florida.

In another experience with the chocolate machine, Paul was carrying the machine down a flight of stairs into a basement cafeteria for a demonstration. Somehow he lost his footing and fell down most of the flight of steps, spilling chocolate drink all over himself. He arrived for the demonstration a walking advertisement for his product—covered with chocolate—and laughing. No matter what happens, Paul seems to come up laughing. "I took all of these experiences with chocolate machine demonstrations as a sign I shouldn't be in the chocolate business," Paul recalls—still with a laugh.

The experiment with the whipped drink machine was soon complete. Paul had never intended to be in that business; his purpose was to learn about franchising. But while he learned what he wanted to know, he gave a good measure of service to the company that employed him. It was not in keeping with his nature to *take* unless he could *give* in return.

THE MOVE TO WORD, INC.

After he called off his involvement with the drink machines, Paul was ready to go to work for Word, Inc. McCracken tried to get

Paul to move to Waco, but Paul believed that if he could sell Word products in Miami when the company was located in Waco, then the company's products would sell anywhere. He went to work on the new project, developing a package—a presentation—to sell Word products. At the same time, he was recruiting and building a sales organization in Miami to sell the Word line. He tried out his system and refined it until he was satisfied. Then he called McCracken to tell him, "I've got it figured out. I'm ready to come to Waco and take you up on the offer to work out of the home office." As a result, he moved to Waco, Texas, and assumed a position at the head of Word's sales organization. In the ten months he represented Word, Inc., in Miami, he personally sold 400 of their library units, built and trained a productive sales organization and developed a complete marketing system for the products.

The confident young Meyer spent approximately two years working with Word in Waco. He recalled his father's four-year stint as an apprentice to the German cabinet maker and his father's frequent statement, "You must start at the bottom if you wish to know a business." He felt that he was following that paternal advice. Meyer's two-year tenure with Word, Inc., was mutually beneficial. He built the company's national sales organization while he learned the mechanics of the communication business and learned to adapt his sales-training techniques to a nationwide sales organization. He proved first-hand the significance of teaching goal setting to a sales force.

As a salesperson, Meyer encountered few objections that he could not handle in the course of a personal sales presentation. He anticipated possible responses to his pitch and had his answers ready. He also taught his salespeople the techniques of answering objections confidently. He was convinced that overcoming objections was largely a matter of allowing the salesperson's strong self-image to be perceived and respected by the client. With a sly twinkle in his eye, he recalls the client who demurred at the purchase of some religious recordings, saying that he must pray about it. The Meyer response came quickly: "I've already prayed about it. That's why I came to see you." Meyer is always a master of reality—with a sense of humor. But he also meant what he said. He had prayed about his work activities, a habit he still follows.

The time he spent as National Sales Director for Word's Library Program was profitable for both Meyer and the company. On June 20, 1959, President McCracken wrote to Meyer:

> . . . as I review the progress of the company since you joined on August 1, 1958, I find that you have played a substantial role in this spectacular growth.

And indeed he had! During his association with the company, sales increased more than 1,000 per cent; and Meyer's personal income increased to well over $100,000 the last year he was at Word.

LAUNCHING THE DREAM

With the success he had achieved at Word, Paul Meyer felt ready to launch out on his own dream. The real foundation of the developing Meyer philosophy was a carefully considered value system. He had learned that a man could be as rich as Midas and still be as "poor as a church mouse." He knew that the key to true success rested in the value system upon which a life is built—the underpinning of a meaningful life. He was beginning to envision a method to help people develop their latent abilities. He believed in people—in their potential. He deplored the colossal waste that occurred when they failed to utilize their talents—their abilities. With missionary zeal he embarked on his new venture in 1960—Success Motivation Institute, Inc.

CHAPTER FIVE
THE DREAM

If you are not making the progress you would like to make and are capable of making, it is simply because your goals are not clearly defined.

Paul J. Meyer

CHAPTER FIVE

THE DREAM

A NEW BEGINNING

By 1960, Paul Meyer had crystallized his thinking about his dream. He believed in the potential of people; he knew that they possessed undeveloped gifts buried under the pressures and even the boredom of daily life. If a tiny spark could ignite a roaring flame, what marvelous human capabilities might be released by the impact of materials that would motivate people to use their latent talents for success.

On January 16, 1960, Success Motivation Institute, Inc., was launched. In a garage converted into an office, Paul Meyer began building his dream. The surroundings were in sharp contrast to the exciting name of the new company, but Paul knew that this location was temporary. In the company's first few months, he engaged an architect to prepare a picture of the building he hoped to build as the company's headquarters. He hung the picture on the wall and looked at it instead of looking at the depressing reality. He believed in himself and his ability to produce materials that people could use to achieve greater success. And he *knew* he could sell, recruit a sales force, and train other people to sell successfully.

As president of the fledgling company, Meyer started to build an organization. His first employee was John Cook, Jr. John's wife Sarah had been Paul's secretary while he was at Word, Inc., and Paul had supported and encouraged Sarah when John was struck down by polio. John spent long months in an iron lung, and doctors gave Sarah little encouragement to believe he could ever leave the lung, much less work again. But John was a fighter, and he was determined to live a productive life. When Paul asked him to join SMI, John Cook was still far from strong, but he seized the opportunity to prove himself. The

Paul in Army uniform.

Paul Demonstrating calisthenics to Army recruits.

Success Motivation Institute's first office.

Paul with his collection book on his first insurance job.

company was so new when John joined it that his long service has become a source of company pride for other officers. At the annual company awards meetings held to recognize employee service, John Cook is always credited with one-half year longer service than Paul Meyer.

THE FIRST PRODUCTS

The first product of the new company was a 33 rpm record, a condensation of the book *Think and Grow Rich* by Napoleon Hill. From the Combined Registry Company owned by W. Clement Stone, Paul acquired the right to produce and market the recorded condensation. Mr. Stone was the president of Combined Insurance Companies of America. He had used the philosophy of Napoleon Hill to help build his company. He was glad to share these concepts with others through this new media. He was also happy to demonstrate his confidence in Meyer and the new company. Stone had earlier published a three-part story about Paul in his magazine, *Success Unlimited.*

Paul found a company in California to press the records and another company to print the record jackets. He and John Cook set up a two-man assembly line to pack and ship the records they sold through advertising. The first 500 records were sold to Zig Ziglar who is now a nationally known motivational speaker.

As the number of orders grew, several other records were added to the catalog. This early catalog included famous speeches and condensations of books that are now recognized as classics in the field of personal development:

Acres of Diamonds by Russell Conwell

I Dare You by William Danforth

As a Man Thinketh by James Allen

The Richest Man in Bayblon by George S. Clason

The Greatest Salesman in the World by Og Mandino

Applied Imagination by Alex Osborne

I Can by Ben Sweetland

EXPANSION OF THE PRODUCT LINE

Paul Meyer knew that he had touched a nerve center: people wanted—*needed*—help to develop their potential. In 1963, based on the solidity of this experience, he put together the company's first full motivation and goal-setting program. This program, *Your Personal Success Planner®*, discussed success factors such as self-image, communication skills, motivation and goal setting. Printed scripts of the narration were supplied to allow reading and note-taking along with listening to the recording. To enhance marketing, the package was made available with a portable battery-operated record player for use in the car.

The format Meyer chose for SMI programs was a printed manual with recordings of each lesson script. The most innovative element of the program was the *Plan of Action* volume that Meyer had devised over a period of years. This volume provides the impetus for action that is needed by most people.

The use of both printed and recorded presentations of content was an innovative approach providing double benefits for the user. The use of recordings makes it easy for users to gain the helpful effect of spaced repetition. New ideas—especially when they deal with changing long-established habits—are not easily internalized the first time they are introduced. Repeated listening to the recordings gives the added input necessary for one to absorb information and decide to act upon it. Reading, while faster than listening, requires one's full attention. Listening, on the other hand, works even when one is busy with automatic chores like dressing, or driving. It also makes good use of time while commuting or waiting.

The second advantage of the double format is the impact of multisensory perception. The emotional appeal of the printed page is different from that of the spoken word. When both approaches are employed, the program user has the benefit of both. The provision for writing in the *Plan of Action* and for making notes in the Lesson Manual adds the use of the muscular sense or sense of touch to the visual and auditory senses already employed. This original format proved so effective that it has been retained for all Success Motivation Institute programs through the years. The only change made has been a switch from records to cassette tapes when this new technology became common.

The innovative *Plan of Action* volume included in this first program has become the hallmark of all SMI programs. The *Plan of Action* had slowly evolved from Meyer's own personal goal-setting activities over a number of years. His long interest in motivating salespeople and helping them to set goals that would inspire them to achievement had demonstrated to him how difficult it is for many people to apply the principles of goal setting to their own dreams. They need a boost to get started—something tangible that they believe they can use. The *Plan of Action* proved to be that tool.

Paul Meyer was twenty years ahead of his time. SMI products were the very first on the market to provide a format for developing a complete written goals plan. Others had suggested setting goals, but no one had previously offered a format that would help people break the procrastination barrier and actually begin the job of writing out a personal goals plan. People who have used the SMI *Plan of Action* hail it as the key to overcoming that major hurdle of getting started. It gives them the needed belief in the value of written goals and the confidence that they can develop and use a personal goals program.

The publication of the *Personal Success Planner* made it possible for Success Motivation® Institute to become a franchise company. There was now a product that would allow a distributor to build a sales organization through which both distributor and sales representatives could earn viable incomes. Meyer immediately began to build a group of salespeople in the home office to reach potential franchisees and present the SMI opportunity to them. At the same time, he had to recruit and train a group of sales managers to work with the new franchisees and help them build their businesses. His previous experience in recruiting and training sales organizations gave him the expertise he needed. For several years, Meyer personally managed distributors in the field while teaching people in the home office how to be effective sales managers. He was also active in the recruitment of new distributors and taught the process to the development staff he had recruited.

For a number of years, even before he established Success Motivation Institute, Meyer had been collecting research materials and making plans for writing a comprehensive program of motivation and goal setting. Over the years, he had discussed this long-range project with his mother, the one person who had always been a source of inspiration and encouragement. She was certain he could write such a course, and she promised to help. For many years, Isabelle Meyer had been an avid reader, and she had saved little bits and pieces—as well as books and articles—that appealed to her. She had, for years, been sending such items to Paul, and he had saved them. They now became important sources of illustrations and indications of basic research sources that Paul secured and studied. Isabelle's interest in the subject of motivation and personal development never waned. Until her death, she regularly sent Paul all sorts of clippings, quotations, books, and articles she found on these subjects.

The result of Paul Meyer's painstaking research and writing was the *Dynamics of Personal Motivation,* first published in 1968. This program was quickly recognized as the most outstanding practical work on the subject of personal motivation available to average individuals. Comparable material was available only in academic texts, heavy with theory, statistics and technical language, and light on practical help for application to daily needs. But these academic materials clearly support and validate the concepts Meyer had formulated through his own experience and observation.

The *Plan of Action* was carefully revised and adapted to complement this new, more extensive program. The *Dynamics of Personal Motivation* has maintained its popularity since its introduction. It has been translated from English into four additional languages—Japanese, Portuguese, French, and German—and has been extensively distributed in almost every English speaking country in the world. It is now in its third edition, with more than twenty printings in English alone.

Meyer next turned his attention to the field that, from the standpoint of personal experience, he knew best—selling. He systematized his vast practical knowledge of selling to produce two programs for professional salespeople: the *Dynamics of Creative Selling* presents basic sales skills with suggestions for developing the character traits that make those skills most effective. With the addition of the *Action Planner for Salespeople,* a special adaptation of the *Plan of Action,* the program has become a full-scale approach to success in sales.

The second sales program from Meyer's pen is the *Sales Manager's Motivation Program.* This program captured Paul's extensive experience in recruiting, training and motivating a sales organization. The *Plan of Action* provided the necessary help for a sales manager—newly appointed or experienced—to establish a program for achievement of both personal goals and career goals.

Goal setting
is the strongest
human force
for
self-motivation.

Paul J. Meyer

EXPANDING HORIZONS IN PRODUCT

From childhood, Meyer had been taught to develop all his talents, to use all his abilities, and to develop interests in every area of life. As a consequence, he emphasized in the *Plan of Action* the need for setting and pursuing goals that would lead to development of a well-rounded life. He included in the *Plan of Action* separate sections for setting goals in six areas of life: physical, mental, social, spiritual, financial, and family life.

Meyer is careful to avoid imposing his own values and priorities on any program user, but he repeatedly emphasizes the importance of the individual's examining every facet of life and establishing priorities and goals that fulfill one's own personal needs. Attesting to the wisdom of this approach are thousands of letters from program users who recount their experiences in self-discovery. Some who acquired an SMI program hoping to make financial gains report that they experienced even greater rewards as they were inspired to set and achieve goals in family and home development, in social activities, or in spiritual growth. Others who were primarily interested in making life simpler and less stressful reached that goal and also enjoyed a corresponding gain in income.

His intense concentration on sales materials did not blind Meyer to the need for other types of motivation programs. In the mid 1960's, he met Dr. J. Clifton Williams, an industrial psychologist, who had practical experience in industrial management along with university teaching and administrative experience. Dr. Williams, who has been associated with Baylor University in various capacities as Chairman of the Psychology Department, Dean of the Graduate School, Administrative Vice-President, and Professor of Management, agreed to help with some programs designed specifically for use in companies. He wrote the original editions of the *Dynamics of Supervision* and the *Dynamics of Motivational Management*.

The outstanding background in both academic and practical areas that Dr. Williams possessed brought ready acceptance and credibility to these new products of the company. To both programs was added an adaptation of Meyer's *Plan of Action* to help program users incorporate the principles and ideas they gained from programs into their daily activities—in their personal lives as well as in their careers.

NEW SALES DIVISIONS

The new materials attracted a large number of new distributors. It soon became apparent that the expansion of the product line, while meeting the needs of various types of clients, had made it impossible for one distributor to handle the entire range of materials. It was too much to know, and too much inventory to maintain. In 1965, a new sales division was established as a part of Success Motivation Institute. Called Leadership Motivation Institute, it was responsible for the marketing of the management and supervisory programs. Later, a new program, the *Dynamics of Personal Leadership,* was added to the product line. LMI began to develop expertise in marketing to people in companies, helping them to meet their need to improve professional productivity.

When LMI was begun, distributors already in SMI continued to market the original personal motivation and sales programs. Achievement Motivation Institute was the new name given to this group of distributors. Both LMI and AMI were made departments of the parent company, Success Motivation Institute, Inc.

GROWING PAINS AND GROUP SALES

All throughout the 1960's, the company struggled to keep up with the demand for its products. Providing the necessary cash flow to recruit new distributors, produce new products, and expand home office facilities was sometimes a difficult task. It was at this time that Paul Meyer drew on his experiences in insurance sales when he used group meetings to sell policies. He worked with distributors and with old insurance contacts to set up groups to whom he could sell SMI programs.

On one occasion in 1964, Meyer was asked to speak at the Insurance School of Purdue University. The agreement was that instead of giving him a fee, he would be allowed to "sell" the audience. He made his presentation to the forty-eight people present, but no one seemed inclined to buy. Then he tried injecting "emotional stories." Still no sale. He looked over his audience to find *one* person who appeared to be a leader and also seemed moderately receptive; he directed his full attention to that one prospect—and even exerted pressure. He was sold! "The others were like dominoes—twenty-four of the forty-eight bought programs." After the session was over, his friend Hal Nutt, Director of the Graduate School of Life Insurance Marketing at Purdue, asked Paul, "Are you OK?"

The answer was, "Sure I'm OK. Why?"

"Well, you were under a lot of pressure!"

"You'd better believe I was," replied the super-salesman. "John Cook [then General Manager at SMI] sent me to this meeting because we had to pay bills at the company, and he told me not to come back without the sales."

Hal became apologetic. He and Paul were sitting in Hal's small foreign convertible in the midst of a snow storm at the airport waiting for Paul's flight back to Waco. He explained that—mostly as a joke—he had invited a group of people from the Psychology Department and the School of Business to come to Paul's session. He told them that Paul was the greatest salesman he had ever observed, and he wanted them to see him in action. So he told them that no matter what Paul did, they shouldn't buy—just to see how he would handle the situation. Now that he realized just how important the sales were to Paul, he was sorry he had made it so difficult for him. He went on to tell Paul that what he had done under the circumstances was miraculous.

Because Hal Nutt had encouraged the audience to resist Paul's presentation, he was doubly curious to hear what those who did buy SMI programs would say later about their purchase. Subsequent interviews revealed a uniform high level of satisfaction with the product they had purchased.

Other people are often astounded by the stories of Paul Meyer's group sales, but one experience still amazes even Paul. At a convention of salespeople, he had been given fifteen minutes of *selling time* in lieu of a speaker's fee. When money was tight at SMI, he often made this offer to a group who solicited his services. (He knew he could bring in far more money that way!) As a part of their coverage of the convention, the local newspaper sent a reporter to interview Paul the night before the presentation was scheduled. Paul quickly became aware of his guest's aversion to salespeople as a class; so he brusquely told the reporter to come to the meeting and pay his fee if he wanted a story.

Paul was the last speaker on the program, and he had planned to use spectacular showmanship to reach the audience of 2,500 salesmen. As one part of his presentation, he had mounted a large pane of glass in a frame on the platform. As he told the audience of the need to break out of old habit patterns and move on to new goals, he threw a baseball through the glass. He used several other gimmicks, also. But as the *piece de resistance* he had hired twenty-five models dressed in smart business suits. Tom Norfleet, then a member of the SMI home office executive staff, had come to the convention with Paul and had trained the models to pass out packets and sales order forms. But without Paul's knowledge, Tom had also offered the models a contest among themselves—a sizeable prize to the model who secured the most signed sales orders.

Paul made his clear-cut, forceful presentation; then he almost fell from the platform! He saw one girl "sit on a guy's lap and run her fingers through his hair. I *had* to do something," recalled Paul. So he asked, "Are we taking this thing to an extreme? Just exactly *how* are these girls *making* these sales?" The crowd started laughing—then became hysterical. Paul reacted quickly and made an instant adjustment in the showmanship scheme he had planned. In what seemed to be an attempt to compete with the models, he sailed 300 one-dollar bills out into the audience. That sent the salesmen scrambling—they are always out to collect every dollar they can.

The upshot was that Meyer sold programs to 125 people. On a plane the next morning, Paul read the local paper. "Themselves Master of the *Foot in the Door Technique* Met the Master Salesman Himself," blared the headline! Amazed, Paul read the story, for he recalled the newsman sitting in the audience, submerged in hostility. But his presentation had evidently won over the reporter. Paul concluded, "I guess he'd rather like *one* salesman and keep hating the rest."

Paul recalls other group sales, too. Once he appeared in Denver, Colorado, with Charles Roth, the author of twenty-seven books on salesmanship, and sold eighty out of eighty in that audience. Roth said in a later interview that Meyer's presentation was the best he had ever seen. On another occasion, Paul sold all forty-nine people at a meeting of American Income Life salespeople in Indianapolis, Indiana. He set up the sale by arranging in advance with the president of the company, Bernard Rapoport, to set up a payroll deduction plan. Rapoport became another of Paul's long-time friends.

Paul Meyer has always been fascinated by group reaction and mass appeal. He learned to "read" a group and choose an approach that would help individuals recognize their need to develop more of their

Successful
people
are motivated
by
successful results.

Paul J. Meyer

potential. These early group-selling experiences eventually led to the development of SMI's training materials for group sales. Some distributors have become capable group sellers and have been able to build large, profitable distributorships through this method that maximizes their time and gives them access to larger numbers of people who can benefit from using SMI programs.

OTHER CONCERNS—PERSONAL AND PEOPLE

One of Paul Meyer's life-long concerns has been maintaining good health. And he goes about it with the same intensity that marks all his activities—with clearly defined goals, a program to follow, and dedication to the task. Once during the 1960's, he returned to Waco from a vacation in Acapulco with a pain in his chest. Chest pains certainly were not in his plan of action; so he went to consult a cardiologist, who rushed him to the hospital before he could give the physician any details about the onset of his condition. Speedily he was hooked up to an electrocardiogram machine, given blood thinners, and then placed under an oxygen tent. Every time he tried to talk, he was told to be quiet and save his strength. All he really wanted to tell *someone* was that he had been sailing when the main rope broke while he was quite a distance out in the ocean. He was forced to hang onto the rope *like this* (with arms extended over his head) for about three hours. A cleat had broken and he had to maneuver the craft back to the bay—about ten miles—from that cramped position.

Although no further symptoms developed, Paul was kept in the hospital for complete bed rest. His doctor told him he had a serious heart condition and would never again be able to work or to engage in any sort of exercise. In true "do-it-yourself style," Paul sent his secretary to the library for books on heart attacks. He collated the information from a number of authorities and learned that most heart attacks are traceable to heredity, obesity, excess fat in the diet, no exercise, smoking, alcohol or stress. Since none of these factors was a problem in his case, he decided he had no cause for worry.

With what he had learned at his finger tips, he decided to debate the subject with his doctor. The doctor was annoyed with Paul's "amateur research." He repeated his opinion that Meyer would never be able to work again. Grudgingly, he agreed to refer Paul to another specialist for a second opinion and made an appointment at the famous DeBakey Clinic in Houston for Paul to have a heart catheterization examination. When the time came for the appointment, Paul was already feeling well. The admitting physician spent two hours taking an exhaustive medical history and conducting an examination and tests. At the end of that time, he leaned back in his chair, laughed and said, "Anybody who exercises like you do, eats what you do—it's probably just a strain. There's no real need for a catheterization." Paul agreed but decided to go ahead with the test for absolute proof.

The surgeon who performed the catheterization presented Paul with his first cause for worry. The doctor was seriously obese, markedly nervous, and chain smoking. Paul relaxed on the table and began to whistle quietly. When the surgeon asked why, Paul explained that he felt relaxed and wanted the surgeon to feel calm, too. The report indicated that the Meyer blood vessels were "big enough to float a battleship." This good news was reported by the admitting doctor who had already decided Paul had no real problem. Paul grinned, and told him he should advise the surgeon to "see a doctor" because he was a prime candidate for a heart attack. Sadly, the following week Paul heard that the surgeon had died of a massive heart attack.

In the midst of his initial concern about his own condition, Paul was still interested in other people. While he waited in the hospital in Waco for the initial verdict of the doctors, he had a visit from Sister Austin, Director of Providence Hospital. Sister Austin made it a habit to call on all patients, despite the multiplicity of her duties. When she came to see Paul, he turned attention to her needs. "You've been working too hard," he admonished. She confessed that her burdens were heavy. Paul, with his sharp insight into people, summed up the problem. "You have such a strong Christian ethic about fulfilling your responsibilities in running this hospital that your conscience hurts if you don't *do everything*. I have a suggestion for you. Make three files for your desk. The first one is the *Imperative* file. In it, put a list of everything that you *must* do today—without fail—and all the papers that are associated with those items. Every day, begin work on these items—one at a time. The second file you need is an *Important* file for all the things you will do today if there is time. When the *Imperative* items are complete, start on this list and do as many as you can.

"The third file is the really good one. It's *Things I Never Intend to Do*. When you get a request for something you don't want to do or don't need to do, put it in that file. Then forget it."

Sister Austin came in the next day—whistling! She smiled, "I think I'll go fishing. I have on my desk an *Imperative* file, an *Important* file, and the greatest file in the world—*Things I Never Intend to Do.*"

CONTINUING COMPANY GROWTH

It was good for SMI that Paul Meyer was a real human dynamo who valued good health and worked at keeping it. The first decade of the company's history is largely the story of his personal activities. With a small staff and a rapidly growing business, it was up to Paul to fill many roles. With the launching of the franchise program came a pressing need for publicity that would build an image for the company—one that would attract the capable people who were needed as franchisees. Paul mapped out a two-pronged strategy: personal appearances all over the nation and publicity in print.

With characteristic thoroughness, Paul organized a sales promotion department in SMI charged with locating publications that would be willing to print something that would help make the SMI name known. Several pieces about Paul and SMI had already appeared. As early as November of 1964, when Paul was thirty-seven, Paul Rosenfield wrote a scintillating four-page feature story for the Sunday *Dallas Times Herald Magazine*—"Meyer's Magic Method—a sparkling success story of the incredible young man who became a millionaire at twenty-seven 'under his own steam'!" Photographer Andy Hanson captured the Meyer vitality and charm in a series of photographs. The journalist wrote:

> . . . this dynamo. . . has done far more with words than Noah Webster. And he's also done more with voice sound than Tallulah Bankhead.

But Paul was more interested in letting people know about SMI and the contribution it could make to their success than he was in gaining personal notoriety. He began to write articles about various facets of selling, about motivation, goal setting, and success. The sales promotion department soon was receiving a flood of requests for Paul J. Meyer articles. The articles appeared in all kinds of journals—sales magazines, journals for sales and business people, company and industry publications. More than two hundred such articles had been published by the mid 1970's.

The second portion of the publicity plan—personal appearances—was more arduous. The name of Paul J. Meyer soon became widely known, and SMI was always coupled with it. Paul undertook speaking engagements all over the United States, and even in a number of other countries in the world. In almost no time at all, he found himself with far more invitations than he could fill. He spoke before all kinds of sales groups—in-house company training sessions, conventions, sales managers, and industry-wide sales groups. He made short motivational speeches and held half- and full-day seminars. He also made it a point to speak to as many as possible of the training schools held in Waco, Texas, for the company's distributor organization. The insurance industry still remembered Paul, and many of his public appearances were before insurance groups. As a result, the insurance world has been one of SMI's best sources for both clients and distributors.

INTEREST IN TIME MANAGEMENT

True to the teachings of his childhood, Paul looked for ways to gain maximum benefits from the many public appearances he made. He decided that if he had to spend all that time and energy traveling, he would make it pay several ways. So he used speaking opportunities to develop, test, and refine new ideas for material that could be used later in new SMI programs. Paul had long been interested in effective time management. He had read, studied, and practiced every suggestion he could find about better time management from his earliest days in selling. He had always taught his salespeople how to maximize their time as one of the best means of increasing income. It was natural for him to talk about time management. He developed both a speech and a full-length seminar on the subject of time management. The seminar was given over a hundred times. The result was that he became even more dedicated to his belief in the importance of good time management and determined that every SMI course would include some information on this vital subject. Eventually he authored two full-length major programs on the subject of time management.

NEW FACILITIES TO MEET NEW NEEDS

As the product line grew, the need for a shorter and faster supply became critical. Pressing records in California, shipping them to Texas, and reshipping them all over the world was both cumbersome and expensive. Contracting for printing, especially after the need expanded to include program texts as well as record jackets, was unsatisfactory from the standpoint of both controlling and scheduling. Paul and John Cook put their heads together to see what they could do about the problem. So they bought a printing press.

Of course, neither of them knew anything about printing, but they reasoned that they had not known anything about selling until they tried it—or running a corporation, or shipping a product. Surely they could learn. There was bound to be an instruction manual, and they could read—couldn't they? They paid $3,500 for the first press. Gene Mason, a pilot who had frequently flown Paul to sales meetings, took the job of running the press. When the first big job came off the press, they were all dismayed to find that the only way to read the pages was to hold them up to a mirror. Somehow, the image had been reversed. That was when they decided it would be good business to hire a qualified professional printer to run the press.

John Cook took on the job of managing the printing operation. In 1962, a subsidiary company, Advertising and Marketing Associates, Inc., was chartered. Not only does it produce all of the printed materials needed by SMI, it also serves the entire state of Texas. It has grown consistently—almost explosively—since its inception and is now the largest graphic arts center in Central Texas.

An additional subsidiary company was established in 1970 to manufacture cassette tapes. Creative Communications, Inc., now has a completely modern facility for recording and cassette duplication that produces all the cassette tapes marketed by the various SMI companies as well as a large volume of work for outside clients.

Later on, in 1979, Vinyl Products, Inc., was started to manufacture the vinyl binders and cassette caddies needed to package the company's products. This company, too, has become an important supplier for clients throughout the Southwest.

Perhaps the most important change affecting company organization and operation was the decision to become a public company. In August, 1969, Success Motivation Institute, Inc., became a publicly-held company with shares traded in the Over-the-Counter Market.

The initial sale of stock provided much-needed capital for expansion of plant facilities and product research and development. In subsequent years the market demand for the stock fell, and the Meyer family bought back the majority of the shares.

While the national and international sales organization grew by leaps and bounds, the home office staff was forced to grow to keep pace—and that meant new buildings. The first permanent home office building was constructed at 5000 Lakewood Drive in Waco, Texas. Soon after the printing company was established, the first manufacturing plant was built on Valley Mills Drive. Both of these buildings have been enlarged and remodeled numerous times. Still, more room was needed. Seven different buildings are now required to house the home office staff and the operation of all the subsidiary companies required to produce and manufacture products, warehouse and ship orders, and provide the support services necessary for serving distributors and clients.

CHAPTER SIX

SMI AROUND THE WORLD

Grow we must...
and the dynamics
of human growth
is change.

Paul J. Meyer

CHAPTER SIX

SMI AROUND THE WORLD

EXPANSION OF THE DREAM

From the very inception of his dream, Paul Meyer had an overwhelming desire to help people "everywhere" learn about the power of goal setting and personal motivation. The founding of SMI intensified his desire. As he proved that the products he was developing actually worked to change people's lives, his sense of mission, tempered by good business judgment, grew even stronger. He knew objectively that the small business he had established was not equipped to handle rapid expansion into various foreign markets. But the dream would not go away.

Always one to enjoy a good joke, Meyer loves being asked how SMI began to move into markets outside the United States. With a perfectly straight face, he begins by saying that he conducted a "highly sophisticated market research" project that started the ball rolling. The creative idea came from his memory of a story his mother had impressed upon him in his childhood—the story of Johnny Appleseed, the simple pioneer who planted apple seeds everywhere he traveled so that those who followed him might enjoy the fruit. Paul noticed, as he traveled, that people often read the magazine that the airline provided for each passenger. Many even took the magazines with them when they reached their destinations. An airlines magazine would be a good place to "plant a seed."

The result of that idea was a $600.00 advertisement in the *Pan American Clipper* magazine directed toward possible distributors of SMI programs outside the United States. That ad constituted the entire "sophisticated market research." Paul placed the ad but by the time it was actually in print, he had dismissed it from his mind.

Amazingly, within days of its appearance, inquiries began to pour in from all over the world—especially from Latin America, South Africa, Australia, and Europe. People everywhere were eager to have access to success materials. From this small *seed,* the world-wide business has grown.

THE LAW OF ATTRACTION

One of Meyer's firmest beliefs is in the operation of the law of attraction. He believes that one who sets goals, devises a plan to achieve them, and then becomes dedicated to their attainment magnetizes the condition that is desired. What others call coincidence, he sees as the normal working of a natural law. Focusing on a goal effectively opens one's eyes to opportunities that others often overlook, attracts people who are ideal associates, and makes available all the resources necessary to success.

In just such a manner, Paul Meyer's goal to found a company dedicated to "motivating people to their full potential"—worldwide—has attracted a number of people uniquely suited to that task. It is these people that Meyer counts as the source of his greatest enjoyment of the international business. Their diversity is typical of the character of the whole company; they are bound by a common desire to achieve their own personal goals and to assist clients to reach their goals.

It was not just the advertisement that brought inquiries. Some of the stories connected with foreign expansion are almost unbelievable. In one instance, a client who had purchased an SMI program in the United States took the program to the Phillippines where it was later stolen. The program eventually found its way to Hong Kong and was sold to Michael Lombardi, an American who lived in Japan. He used the program, and immediately set a goal to meet Paul J. Meyer and become a part of the SMI business. Some time later, he made a trip to the United States and sought out Meyer. As a result, Lombardi became the distributor of SMI programs in Japan. He supervised the translation of the first programs marketed in Japan, and then recruited and trained a sales organization. Lombardi had been associated for a number of years with cultural exchange programs that involved the production of Japanese theater, dance, and film all over the world. This activity had given him a broad understanding of Japanese culture, and he firmly believed that the Japanese people would eagerly accept the concepts of personal success and motivation presented in SMI programs although many people in the company predicted that cultural differences would be insurmountable. Experience proved Lombardi's judgment to be correct.

From a path almost as complicated came Daniel Rubinski. In the mid-1970's SMI held a world convention in Acapulco, Mexico. Paul had been busy almost every minute of the several days he had been in Acapulco, and finally decided to take a little time to relax by the pool with his friend Michael Lombardi. They noticed that only one person was swimming in the pool. In keeping with his level of self-confidence—as well as his spirit of fun and bravado—Paul told Mike that since there seemed to be only one prospect in sight, he would recruit that one. He swam out to the man and initiated a conversation. "I noticed that you were reading a self-improvement book a little while ago. I'm in that business." It turned out that the "prospect" was Daniel Rubinski from Argentina, the owner of several large department stores. He was in Mexico visiting his brother, a famous Mexican movie star who was an enthusiastic SMI program user. The brother had sent Daniel an SMI program, and Daniel, too, had used it. One goal he had set was to come to the United States, meet Paul, and represent SMI in Argentina. Several weeks later, as a result of that meeting, he and his family came to Waco and signed a contract to market SMI programs in Argentina. He was active in the business for some years and is now retired.

Another member of the international organization who has made a satisfying career in SMI is Ted Kemper, the General Director of SMI of Canada. Ted first joined SMI in January, 1969, as a distributor. Prior to that time, he had worked as a driver of a catering truck. By his own admission, Ted was withdrawn and shy. He had left school at the age of fourteen, and he felt that the lack of adequate education was a serious obstacle to his success. But association with SMI people and SMI programs changed Ted's outlook on life. He realized that his success as a distributor would depend on what he was willing to do for himself. The desire to succeed in his business forced him to get an education; and he set to work systematically to do just that. He also found it necessary to change some of his personality traits—to become less shy and withdrawn. He set goals to be more involved with people and to interact with them more effectively. His success in achieving these goals led to his selection just three years later as General Director for SMI's entire European operation. After two and a half years in this position, Kemper and his wife Klara decided to return to Canada, and he was appointed General Director in that country in September, 1974. He still holds this position and operates a large and profitable business among both the English- and the French-speaking populations of that country.

Ted Kemper regards Paul Meyer as a real "straight shooter" in all his business operations. "I know," says Ted, "that when Paul says something, he stands behind it, even if it hurts him. A handshake is enough of a contract with Paul for my own feelings of security. We have a written contract only so others will know what we have agreed in the event that something happens to either or both of us." Ted Kemper has used SMI programs and concepts to build a better life for himself. In addition to inspiring him to gain needed education, use of SMI materials produced dramatic increases in his skills and achievement level in all other areas of life, including making him a better husband and father.

The desire for economic success was the force that first attracted Hei Arita to SMI. Hei Arita had worked for a number of years in various managerial positions with different Japanese airline companies, but he was dissatisfied with the level of advancement he was making. In 1969, he happened to see a small advertisement in a newspaper and visited SMI's office in Tokyo to investigate. He was excited about the company's whole concept and was eager to become a sales associate, but he lacked the ¿100,000 (about $500 U.S.) he needed to purchase the necessary training materials and sales kit. He finally found a family friend who helped him arrange a loan. As soon as he began to market SMI programs, he also began using a program personally—a practice he still follows. His first discovery was that the six areas of his life were badly out of balance, and he set about the task of developing a more well-rounded life through setting goals for personal growth in all areas.

Hei Arita's first goals were financial because he felt this was the most pressing area of need for him; he also knew that achieving financial goals would give him the needed resources to reach other goals as well. He set up some progressive goals for saving and investing his money—first ¿100,000, then ¿1,000,000, ¿10 million and ¿100 million. He took seriously the suggestion made in the program to visualize goals. He went to his banker and—after persistent requests—was allowed to have his picture taken in front of a table holding stacks of currency amounting to ¿80 million, which was all the bank had available that day. He looked at his picture frequently and visualized himself owning that money as a result of his own earnings. Those first financial goals have all been reached and Hei Arita has set a number of new challenging goals for his business.

His interest in becoming financially independent did not keep Arita from giving attention to other areas of life. He regularly gives a part of his income to churches, the Japanese Red Cross, relief for refugees, and other charitable causes. His contacts with clients have gained him social credibility; he has made friends among professional people and executives of leading companies. He has also benefited from goals to improve his family life—an area that he had largely neglected in his earlier years. In 1982, Hei Arita was made head of the total marketing organization in Japan. At that time, Paul Meyer had come to Japan to attend the annual convention and told Hei Arita that he hoped to enjoy a good friendship with him for at least thirty years to come. Arita determined that he would do his part to make that wish come true; so he set some physical fitness goals to improve his health and fitness. Since that time, he has regularly practiced Yoga twice a week and played golf once a week.

In 1984, Hei Arita became president of PJM of Japan, Ltd., the company licensed to distribute Paul Meyer's programs in the Japanese language. Arita is proud that this company is the only one in the world that has permission to use Meyer's name as its company name. His goals for the future of the company are already outlined all the way to the year 2000, and the computer system he installed includes software specifically designed to support the needs of a company the size he sees in his goals. Other goals for the future include his desire to have four generations of his family living together in his house. He and his wife Toyoko have two daughters and a young son. As he looks back over seventeen years of association with Paul J. Meyer, Hei Arita speculates that "If I did not have a chance to meet SMI and Paul J. Meyer, my life would have been completely different."

UNITY IN DIVERSITY

Paul Meyer's dream is still in the *becoming* stage. But enough success has been realized that his belief and his determination know no bounds. One of the most satisfying experiences he has enjoyed is the spirit of unity achieved by members of the SMI family in spite of the

Opportunities are everywhere for one who understands and uses

self-motivation.

Paul J. Meyer

great diversity found among them and the conditions under which they work in various parts of the world.

It is interesting to see the different types of people who are attracted to SMI. The top officers in the company come from all sorts of prior professions. They include an engineer, a professional baseball player, a C.P.A., an insurance agent, a meat cutter in a packing plant, the business manager of a church, a teacher, and an executive of a consumer loan company. Salespeople of all kinds find that the company offers unusual opportunities for success in sales and sales management.

The glue that binds together this unusual group of people is evident whenever they gather. It is a spirit of belief in and commitment to one another and to the achievement of challenging goals that makes SMI successful. Outsiders sometimes see SMI people as materialistic, too interested in money and recognition. And certainly there are those who are attracted to the company and its products through the desire for financial gain and personal recognition; but those are not the ones who stay for any length of time. It is also true that many of the officers and distributors have achieved financial success through their SMI careers, but these same people have exhibited even greater achievement in personal growth, community service, and leadership in other areas of life.

VICTORY IN ADVERSITY

One of the principles Paul Meyer learned from his mother was that the greatest victories are those won over adversity. She taught him that problems and difficulties were God's gifts designed to push him to discover new talents and abilities that he could use in finding solutions. Over the years, Paul has refused to become discouraged by the adversity that others call problems, troubles, or failures. He prefers to call them opportunities. The goal to serve people has brought SMI its share of such "opportunities."

The first creative opportunities Meyer faced were roadblocks that would have stopped anyone less committed to a dream or less determined to succeed. His personal resources formed the first capital for the new company, but these were soon exhausted and he sought expansion capital through local banks and other financial institutions. He ran into solid walls of doubt. The burden of the reaction seemed to be "How do you know anyone wants to buy records that contain condensations of books?" Obviously, Paul's dream lacked credibility in their eyes. But it was real for him. He knew someone would believe in him.

Meyer thought back through his earlier experiences to decide who would believe in him and help him over this hurdle. One name leapt into his mind—W. Clement Stone! Since that day in his youth when Paul had played the waiter to meet Mr. Stone, the two had become fast friends. The older man may have seen in the younger something of his own entrepreneurial spirit and much of his own determination to succeed. He had often told Paul to call him if he ever needed help. So Paul called. Mr. Stone immediately called the Republic Bank in Dallas and talked to Mr. Oren Kite, Senior Vice President of the bank. The bank loaned Paul the money he needed to keep the young company moving toward success. Later when expansion funds were again needed, Mr. Stone endorsed Meyer's note for $200,000.00 at the American National Bank in Chicago. Mr. Stone's willingness to take a risk in his behalf is one of Paul's dearest memories.

When SMI was first begun, cassette tapes were still experimental, and tape players were few in number and expensive. Record players were fairly common in homes, but being tied to home listening meant people could not make maximum use of the recorded information. Meyer searched all over the United States for a portable record player that was battery operated and stable enough to be used in a moving car. Nothing was practical. At last, he located such a player in England. It was called the Wondergram and was designed with an arm that held the playing needle and also clamped the record into place so that the player would operate acceptably while resting on the seat of a car. For several years, the players were imported and sold along with SMI records and later with programs.

Times of adversity have served as the impetus for formation of the manufacturing companies that form the SMI family of companies and that manufacture all of the SMI products. The first such experience came with printing needs. As the product began to expand, Paul met with the printing companies who had been producing the programs to choose some new type fonts and design a new graphic style for a new program. He met with a complete lack of cooperation. "We have always used these type styles for everything we do. There's no need for anything new." This attitude was the final frustation that caused Paul to buy a printing press and start printing his own products. The ultimate benefits were tremendous. The printing company is now the largest complete graphics center in central Texas.

The tape duplicating company came about in a similar manner. When portable tape recorders became numerous enough and low enough in price to be practical, SMI's records were converted to cassette tapes. The master recordings were sent to a company in another state for duplication. After a while, the quality of the recordings declined. It turned out that the tape company had decided that since the tapes for SMI were not music, high fidelity recording was a waste of money. They were salvaging used computer tapes, splitting them into the widths needed for cassettes, and recording over them—all the while charging SMI for new, high quality tape. Paul decided to end the problem once and for all. He bought duplicating equipment and began producing SMI tapes in the building with the printing company. Now the tape company is one of the largest capacity duplicating shops in the region.

Copyrights have proved another type of difficulty to be overcome. For a company whose products consist of ideas and information, a copyright is comparable to a manufacturing company's patent that protects its exclusive right to produce and market a product it has invented. To complicate the matter, the law places on the copyright owner the burden of monitoring the marketplace and initiating a complaint when a violation occurs. The most extensive copyright violation SMI has suffered came when a former leading distributor decided to leave the company and strike out on his own. He immediately published his own programs that closely paralleled Meyer's writings—even lifting long passages word for word. To compound the damage SMI suffered, he also began to contact some of SMI's franchised distributors, offering to sell them programs *just as good* at greatly reduced introductory prices—a tactic designed to lure them away from SMI and form a nucleus for his new company.

Paul had to protect the product. So he made the decision to bring suit. Added to the financial reverses of lost sales and heavy legal expenses was the emotional burden caused by the sense of betrayal. Once again Paul's open trust of people and his willingness to believe in their good motives had resulted in financial loss for him. When the case came to court, the judge ruled in favor of Meyer and SMI—delivering a stern lecture to the culprit. "You are not only guilty of flagrant plagarism," the judge said, "but you made absolutely no attempt to hide your intent. Anyone can see immediately what you have done. It is obvious that you have assumed that justice is blind, and that judges are, too." The outcome was that all of the plagarized material was confiscated and the perpetrator's business dissolved.

Such difficulties have not destroyed Meyer's basic belief in the goodness and potential of people. He firmly believes that people deserve the right to prove what they can and will do, and he refuses to prejudge anyone's ability or commitment. He is also eager to forgive, for he believes that holding grudges or harboring hatred is self-destructive. Some months after settlement of the case mentioned, Paul traveled to the home city of the man involved, called him and invited him and his wife to dinner. He told the couple that he wanted to forgive and forget—preferring to retain the happy memories of a friendship than to hold hostile thoughts and bitterness of spirit.

International copyrights and trademarks have also caused problems. One person who violated SMI copyrights in Ireland finally was sent to prison. A South African man went bankrupt when SMI's copyrights were upheld. Establishment of SMI in Australia was seriously hampered and delayed because one man who was negotiating with SMI for distribution rights promptly registered the SMI copyrights and trademarks in his own name in that country. Through all these "opportunities for creative problem solving" came the proof that adversity can be a blessing. SMI has never lost a copyright suit, and some of the experiences that seemed depressing at the time eventually produced such fortuitous side effects that they turned into real victories. Happily, there seems to be some evidence that, in the interest of promoting international trade, a number of countries are now tightening their trademark and copyright laws to prevent such piracy.

When SMI first became a franchise company, complying with the laws in all the different states appeared to be an complex problem. That problem has now—through meticulous attention to the details of all applicable laws—become merely a massive clerical operation in tending to intricate details—different from state to state. But that arduous task is dwarfed by the problems of marketing in numerous international environments.

The differences in laws from state to state, although sometimes irritating, can be handled by giving careful attention to details. But the variations in international laws are much more difficult. Not only is it difficult to comply with complicated import laws, but the problem is compounded when these laws change from year to year—and change in some countries but not in others—and often without prior notice.

The SMI business is basically the same all over the United States, but the international business frequently demands a different basic business structure in each country. Some countries allow relatively free importation of programs. Others will allow printed materials to be imported, but sound recordings are not allowed—and *vice versa.* Some countries allow importation of neither printed material nor recordings. In these countries, arrangements must be made to manufacture programs there—an approach that introduces the considerations of accuracy and quality control that are normally handled in the Waco plant.

Economic differences in international markets have had a profound effect on the business in different parts of the world. The political and economic unrest in Central America has hampered growth of the business during the 1980's, but SMI distributors are patiently waiting out this period of turbulence. They believe in the business and feel certain that the time will come when they can move forward again. A similar condition exists in Mexico. The repeated devaluation of the peso has made it almost impossible for Mexican citizens to consider investing in a product like an SMI program. Abelardo Maldonado, the SMI General Director who operates the organization in that country, sold his new home and liquidated a large portion of his personal investments to keep the business going. Like Paul, he has learned persistence in adversity. He firmly believes he will regain the prosperous state his business once enjoyed.

Translation and recording of program materials is a continuing problem faced in international marketing. To make sure that translations will be of maximum effectiveness, dynamic equivalents rather than literal word-for-word translations are used. Special care is taken to insure that every translation is accurate and appropriate in every way for the country where it will be marketed. Attention is also given to style and literary acceptability so that every SMI program—in every language—is of the highest possible quality.

Various programs are now being produced in eleven different languages:

English	Spanish	Portuguese
French	Norwegian	Swedish
Danish	Finnish	Italian
German		Japanese

The points of the achievement compass are north, east, south, west and where you are —

Now!

Paul J. Meyer

SMI's products are currently marketed in North, South and Central America, Africa, Europe, Asia, Australia, and island nations in the Caribbean and the Pacific—in more than fifty countries in all.

In the early days of the company, Meyer often tackled cash flow problems by going out into the field and selling programs—usually to large groups. Once when he had made a presentation to a group and closed a large number of sales, a banker in the group asked Paul why he would stoop to selling programs himself. "It is undignified," he said, "for the president of the company to do that."

Paul's reply was characteristic. "If you want to succeed, you do what you have to do, when you have to do it," he said. "I'll do whatever is necessary to build this company—pack boxes, do the selling myself, fix a flat tire. I'm willing to do whatever is necessary to get where I want to go." Such determination reflects the burning desire for achievement, the willingness to work, and the sense of commitment that have always marked Paul Meyer and led to his continued success.

THE PROBLEM-SOLVING FORMULA

Throughout SMI's history, Paul Meyer has approached problem solving with a somewhat unique formula that had its seeds in the teachings of his mother and has attained its full growth in his business and family life. Here is his approach:

1. Thank God for the problem.
   Paul admits that this is sometimes difficult, but he firmly believes that something good will come into his life and experience as a result of the problem. He claims the Biblical promise that "all things work together for good to them that love God." (Romans 8:28) He constantly reminds himself that all things are not "good," but that they can bring good if he uses his God-given creativity to find the best solution. He takes literally the admonition of the Apostle Paul: "The Lord is near; have no anxiety, but in everything make your requests known to God in prayer and petition with *thanksgiving*. Then the peace of God, which is beyond our utmost understanding, will keep guard over your hearts and your thoughts, in Christ Jesus."

2. Write down at least five benefits of the problem.
   From his mother, Paul learned that every adversity has the seed of an equivalent or greater benefit—if you believe it, look for it and work for it. So he writes out the benefits he could enjoy as a result of encountering and solving this particular problem.

3. Make a written plan of action for solving the problem.
   The next step is to write a list of possible actions that could be taken to solve the problem. Writing is important—it captures creative ideas and gives a sense of commitment to taking action.

4. Once all the possible actions are listed, make a choice and act.
   The most impressive list of solutions in the world will never produce success unless someone takes action. Paul evaluates all the possible solutions, chooses the one that appears to be the most likely to produce the desired result, and then immediately implements it.

5. Track progress and make necessary adjustments.
   It sometimes happens that the action step that appears most likely to produce success fails to have the desired result. Success in problem solving—or in any under taking is not automatic. If the first possible solution produces less than the desired result, out comes the list of possible actions again. New possibilities are added, and the process begins again. Sometimes only minor adjustments are needed; at other times an entire approach must be discarded and a new path charted.

This simple, yet powerful, system for solving problems has worked for Meyer in his personal life and in his business. It owes its effectiveness to four of his personal characteristics: (1) Meyer's deep and sincere faith in God and his belief that God intends for life to be good; (2) his willingness to think and act creatively, even when that involves taking risks; (3) his acceptance of personal responsibility for solving his own problems; and (4) his determination and persistence in keeping at the job until the problem is solved.

Two typical experiences show how Paul has effectively used his problem-solving approach. The first occurred in 1975. Paul owned a farm of two hundred acres in Georgia. He decided he would like to sell it and listed it with real estate agents in the area. After two years with no results, one agent told Paul that no farm had been sold in the area for a long time because of the depressed economy of the area. So Paul decided to sell it himself. After the preliminary steps of the problem-solving plan, Paul called an old insurance friend, and together they made a list of all the things they could do to attract enough attention to the farm that they could sell it. Then they moved into action. They sent out direct mail flyers inviting people in the area to a big party at the farm. They advertised in the local paper, and set signs up along the highway inviting passersby to the event. They set up a tent and provided food and music. Then they held an old-fashioned auction. And they sold the farm at a fair price. Paul did want to sell the farm, but he especially enjoyed showing the realtors who said it couldn't be done just how wrong they were.

In a similar experience almost ten years later, Paul managed to sell three resort condos he owned. He had listed them with several realtors, all of whom told him there was no market for condos. Paul refused to believe them. He knew the resort was an excellent one. It offered golf, tennis, and boating, and was located in a beautiful setting. He decided that owning these condos gave him an opportunity to help some people acquire a property that would add to the happiness of their families. So he made it a point to watch the people who came in to rent condos—especially when they had a family. If he saw the same family twice, he introduced himself and told them about his condos for sale. He was able to sell all three condos, one on each of three successive trips he made to the resort with his family—and made over $100,000.00 profit. But the most enjoyable part of all was that he did it while the members of the resort sales staff were sitting in the office talking about how bad business was. "It just goes to prove," Paul says, "that the whole world stands aside for one who knows where he's going. There is always business out there for one who will go for it."

CHAPTER SEVEN

THE LENGTHENED SHADOW

Attitudes
are nothing more
than
habits of thought...

and habits can be

acquired.

Paul J. Meyer

CHAPTER SEVEN

THE LENGTHENED SHADOW

SMI AND ITS CLIENTS

SMI's files contain thousands of letters from people who have used Paul Meyer's programs and found them helpful in various areas of their lives. Meyer considers the stories told in these letters to be proof that all people do indeed possess a great deal of potential for growth and achievement. All that is needed for them to maximize their success is an understanding of their need for systematic goal setting. When this need is met by an SMI program, people are free to use their full potential for success.

The first *Plan of Action* Paul Meyer put together for an SMI program emphasized the need for setting and achieving goals in six areas of life: physical, mental, social, spiritual, financial, and family life. Throughout the years, every *Plan of Action* has continued that emphasis. Stories from clients show a diversity of experiences in setting and reaching goals in each of these six areas.

One of Meyer's favorite stories is that of one man who wrote to say that he had never given much thought to the spiritual area of life before acquiring his SMI program. He began working in his *Plan of Action,* but rejected the idea that he needed to set spiritual goals. As he continued using the program, he frequently heard on the lesson tapes and read in the manual the admonition that every area of life must be considered in a goals program—that for one individual various areas of life—at different times in life—show different levels of *urgency* in the need for growth. But *each* area must be considered and assigned its proper priority based on the individual's own value system. Otherwise, the unresolved priority forms a continuing source of vague uneasiness. This particular client finally decided to fill out the section of the *Plan of Action* devoted to spiritual goals. He explained his motivation for the decision like this: "I decided that since I had spent my hard-earned money for this program, I should get maximum benefit from it—I couldn't afford to waste any part of my money." He went on to tell how the self-examination process in the spiritual section of the *Plan of Action* revealed to him a sense of spiritual void he had not previously recognized. He decided to do something about his spiritual life. He investigated the churches in his area, chose one, and began to take his family to worship. In a short time, he realized that he had long been missing a dimension of life that was now bringing him satisfaction and fulfillment.

Almost everyone who writes SMI to report career or business success as a result of using a program adds comments on achievements in other areas of life also. A recent letter from a Georgia realtor, Bruce E. Weinkauf, begins by recounting his increased achievements in sales: "Within six months. . .I made the largest sale ever made in my office's history. The house I sold had been on the market for three years. . .I have tripled my income this year over last year." Significantly, though, he adds, "My career is not the only area in which I have experienced satisfying results. . .I am eating a healthier diet and feel really good. . .I am experiencing deeper relationships with people. . ."

Walter D. Woodgett, a salesman for IBM, wrote to tell of being in a career slump, close to losing his job. As something of a last resort, he purchased an SMI program and began to use it. "Within four months," he reported, "my sales productivity has rocketed me to the position of top IBM Salesman in the United States within the Biomedical Systems Division. Last month I closed the largest single sales order of the year for Computerized EKG Systems. More important have been the internal changes in my attitude and the increased confidence and belief in myself."

In November, 1984, Paul Meyer attended the convention held for the company's salespeople in Japan. A memorable part of his experience during this visit was the opportunity to meet a number of long-time SMI clients among the Japanese people. Several of them even spoke at the convention. Among the speakers was Mr. Yoshito Igarashi, President of the 1 World Store—a chain of major department stores. The letter Paul received from this client after the convention told more of the story. Yoshito Igarashi was born the son of an impoverished farmer in the north of Japan. His father's low economic status made it necessary for him to drop out of high school to help support the family. In spite of the difficulty experienced in Japan by those without adequate education, he was determined to succeed.

At age seventeen, Igarashi went to work as a day laborer for a construction company. A year later he was a supervisor. At twenty-three, he began to work in a retail store. About that time, he learned about SMI and purchased his first program. For ten years he concentrated his energies on setting goals and becoming a success in his work. He became one of the top key staff members and a stockholder of the company. In 1975, he opened his own business, the 1 World Store, with only three staff members, including himself. Nine years later, he had over 400 employees and his seven stores grossed $100,000,000.00 (U.S.) in sales.

Igarashi had a long-standing goal to meet Paul J. Meyer and express appreciation for the writings that had aided him. When he was invited to meet Meyer and to speak at a session of the convention, Igarashi decided that as a part of his speech he would commit himself to reaching a challenging long-range goal by the year 2000 and that he would share that goal with the audience. He considered most carefully what he would say because he knew he intended to do whatever was necessary to fulfill the promise he would make before this large group of people. He wanted to be positive he could actually reach the goal, but he was equally concerned that it should be a worthy one. The goal he chose to announce was his projection that his stores would realize total retail sales of $2,000,000,000.00 (U.S.) in the year 2000.

When he came to the meeting at which he was to speak, Igarashi was excited to see on display a sample of a new program soon to be introduced in Japan. He was determined that this first copy should be his. He was told that the sample was just for display—that the program was not quite ready for release; but his insistence was so strong that it was decided he could have the sample program at the conclusion of the convention. He was greatly moved to receive the program from the hand of Meyer himself. He announced his goal as he had planned, and in a letter to Meyer the next month, his description of the experience—in his own English—conveys a vivid sense of the emotion he felt: "People's applause made me exciting and dreamed like 2 Billion sales reached already."

Dan Spencer, a Texas realtor, is another program user who found his SMI program valuable in more than his career. In 1977 Dan found himself embroiled in both personal and financial problems. He describes himself at that time as a "real basket case." By chance, he picked up a magazine containing a feature article about using cassette tapes in the car. One phrase stuck with him: "People spend $100.00 a year on hair cuts, but not one cent that goes *into* their heads." He sought out an SMI Distributor and purchased a program. The first benefits he noticed were a marked decrease in stress and a corresponding increase in positive attitude. He goes "back to the basics" every year and works through his programs as though they were new. At the time he began using SMI materials, Dan lived in Illinois. In 1983 he decided to return to his native Texas—he claimed it was to get his feet warm—although it is likely he had other motivations as well. He went into real estate and earned his realtor's license within a few months. His first six months' sales reached over $1,000,000.00. In 1984, his sales topped $2,000,000.00. He now faces the future with excitement and sees no limits to his success.

Francis K. LeClercq was nearing military retirement when he purchased one of Paul J. Meyer's courses. He was too young to think about retiring to idleness, but he had no idea what he wanted to do with his life after military retirement. He hoped the program would help him set some long-range goals. But he found that it had immediate benefits beyond his expectations. He reports: "My daily routine became better organized and much more goal directed. The 'too hard to do' came to the top of the list and perhaps even more important, I began to see how they too could be accomplished. . .I also came to understand that achieving meaningful life goals demanded much more. To reach higher order goals you must go beyond the mechanics of goal setting and increased productivity. The process . . .must be made your own and doing so demands commitment."

Neal R. Altland is Publisher and General Manager of a leading daily newspaper in Ohio. His involvement with SMI programs goes back almost twenty-five years to 1963 when he took out a loan at the bank to purchase his first SMI program. He had been working in advertising sales at the newspaper for a year. His salary was, in his words, "a whopping $55 a week." He was discouraged and considering looking for another job—perhaps with a major metropolitan newspaper. As he began to use the program, he realized that his future was right in his own back-yard—in his own hands—and that it was his responsibility to make things happen.

Altland knew it would be tough to get to the top because he lacked a college degree, but his positive mental attitude and definite goal plan made him confident of success. Within a year he was the top producer on the sales staff, a rating he held as long as he was in sales. In 1970, at the age of 27, he was promoted to Classified Advertising Manager; five years later, he was made Advertising Director. He has continued to rise in the company and to produce outstanding results in every assignment he is given. In 1981 Altland was made General Manager and a year later was given added responsibilities as Publisher. With a proven track record in his career, Neal Altland reflects: ". . .for years I felt ashamed that I had not attended college and acquired a degree. Today, when people ask where I got my degree, I tell them that my 'formal' education was from SMI."

Clients who have used SMI programs are often eager for an opportunity to meet the author. A few even go to great lengths to satisfy their desire to meet Paul Meyer and express their gratitude for the help they have received from using a program. One such client was a man named Henry Tseung, a banker, businessman and entrepreneur from Hong Kong. Already successful in his own right, Mr. Tseung made excellent use of an SMI program to help increase his personal success and to inspire his employees to achieve greater success. One day he showed up in Waco, Texas, and asked to see Meyer.

Mr. Tseung introduced himself, told Meyer about using the program, then in his own limited English, explained his purpose for coming to Waco. "Paul help Henry; now Henry help Paul. Go on with work. I observe." With that, he sat down in Paul's office and, with typical Oriental inscrutability, *observed*. By the next afternoon Henry was ready to *help*. At this time, SMI was just beginning to experience the rapid growth that was soon to elevate it to the status of a major corporation. Since Paul had started SMI by doing everything himself, he was still operating from more or less that same point of view. He was still personally involved in every facet of the business—supervising and approving each project and each piece of work done by everyone in the growing corps of officers and employees.

Mr. Tseung began his *help* by telling Paul: "I think SMI will never be big company. You think Paul must do everything. You tell officers and managers what to do—then add *how* to do. You make them feel little. You not only intelligent person in company. Give people job; let them decide how. Then you look at job. Make little correction if necessary. They get bigger. You get bigger."

Mr. Tseung's principle was not a new concept. Paul knew his people had unlimited potential for achievement. He was committed to that concept. The problem was that it was *his dream* they were work-

Self-motivation

is the power

that raises you

to any level

you seek.

Paul J. Meyer

ing on, and he had unconsciously allowed his obsession with the dream to become possessiveness—to a point that was stretching his physical and emotional capacity beyond the limits of possibility. Paul was grateful for Mr. Tseung's help. Once he admitted to himself that the only way to achieve his dream was to let others help, he became a master of delegation. Now he makes sure that every program designed for use in companies contains information on delegation. He teaches his own company officers and managers to delegate. "Your subordinates," he tells them, "will probably *not* do the job as well as you would do it. They certainly will not do it the *way* you would do it. But if they do it 80% as well as you would, you are ahead of the game. When you have ten people working at 80% of the effectiveness you would most like to see, they can do far more than you could ever do alone—even if you did everything perfectly."

Charlie Pack has been using SMI programs since 1969. In both high school and college, Charlie had been an outstanding success. He was a high school All American basketball selection and earned All Conference recognition in college basketball. After college, Pack wanted to excel in both business and sports. He chose fishing as his main outdoor activity and became the Texas Big Bass Champion in 1961 and Texas Open Champion in 1965. At the same time, he was beginning his career in insurance sales, as he explains it—at the bottom of the pile. That was a real challenge to one accustomed to being on top.

By 1969, Charlie had been in the insurance business for seven years. He was making progress, but he was far from satisfied with the level of his achievement. His income was averaging about $15,000 annually, but he believed in himself and knew that he had the potential to do much better. That's when he heard about SMI. He purchased one of Meyer's programs. Here's how he described its impact on him: "It introduced me to a new way of thinking and I began to gain a new appreciation of what the world has to offer. I began to see the tremendous untapped potential that exists for everyone." Within a few short years, Charlie was thinking in terms of $100,000 as his annual income.

The most exciting concept Charlie Pack absorbed from the program was the belief that he could do anything he put his mind to. That's where he let his creativity take over. He decided he would figure out how to fish and make a living at the same time. So fishing became his favorite method of prospecting for new clients in the life insurance business. Just as some salespeople invest in computers and other business equipment, Charlie has invested in first class fishing equipment including a fishcleaning room and drive-through garage to store his boat. His "client fishing" is now known all over town as "an afternoon of fishing with Charlie." The prospect of the day—along with his whole family—spends several hours on the lake and goes home with a video tape of the trip. Charlie is convinced that word of mouth is the greatest advertising in the world. Since we all like to see ourselves on film, the video tape is the first order of conversation when Charlie's clients have visitors at home. When that video shows the family catching 60 to 200 crappie in one afternoon of fishing, the visitor naturally wants to know all about it. And Charlie's name is introduced to another prospect.

Charlie Pack now spends at least three afternoons a week fishing for prospects—and crappie. One secret to his successful prospecting is that he knows both life insurance and fishing. He knows where to take his prospects to be sure the fishing is good, and he knows how to advise them about insurance needs. Of course, he claims that he has a unique power phrase for closing: SIGN OR SWIM!

Charlie's interests, in addition to insurance and fishing, include leading his own band that plays at dances and parties throughout the Central Texas area. He originally organized the band to supplement his income, but he continues it mainly for fun. His family also gets a lot of attention. His wife Lynn and their four daughters enjoy their home tennis court and the backyard basketball games where Charlie is the coach and Lynn the referee. A person who finds fulfillment in a chosen career, has time to enjoy life, and makes a contribution to the lives of others deserves to be called successful. So Charlie Pack is truly successful—but he is never completely satisfied. He continually sets new goals and accepts new challenges for further growth. He knows that complacency is one step before failure.

THE SMI FAMILY

SMI clients are not the only ones who are excited about the results they achieve through the use of SMI programs. Distributors are enthusiastic about the goals they reach through using the materials they market. Clyde Rosser has been a Distributor in Indiana since the early 1960's. When he talks about his SMI experience, the goals he remembers include family achievements, travel, hobbies, and the enjoyment of association with many SMI home office executives, particularly with Paul J. Meyer. When he lists the memorable events from his SMI career, one that he recalls is the time he had the opportunity to have breakfast with Meyer alone during a training meeting in Waco.

Clyde Rosser's family is a source of pride for him. He and his wife have seven children and eight grandchildren—all of whom have been treated to a strong dose of SMI attitude training. One of the early family goals Clyde set was to have a redhaired daughter who would be crowned queen at high school homecoming. This goal, set before his daughters were born, was realized twice over: two of his daughters, both red heads, were voted homecoming queens, and a blond daughter was a runner up. But Clyde's real pride in his children is based on much less frivolous criteria than beauty and popularity. His SMI business helped him provide ample education for all seven children. The Rosser sons earned college degrees, one from Indiana University, and one from Purdue. Both are doing well in their chosen careers of sales and engineering. The five Rosser daughters are married, and four of them also have significant professional careers. Among them, the seven Rosser children achieved an impressive list of honors and attainments in school and are continuing their winning habits in adult life.

The goals Rosser has achieved include numerous family vacations in exotic resorts such as Waikiki, Acapulco, and the Virgin Islands, topped off by a three-month, around-the-world trip to twenty-six countries—all planned with the help of an SMI *Plan of Action*. One of Clyde's interests is luxury cars; he has purchased more than fifty cars including Cadillacs and Lincoln Town Sedans—all as a part of his personal goals program. Among Clyde's favorite souvenirs of his long association with SMI are letters received from grateful clients whose use of SMI programs brought benefits to them through personal goals achieved and through improved performance of their employees who also had used SMI programs in company groups. He also has a thick file of bulletins and awards notices from SMI featuring his picture, the records he has set, and the awards he has earned—mementos that tell of dedication to a purpose, hard work, and accepting personal responsibility for his own success.

Paul Meyer likes to tell stories about distributors whose use of an SMI program was exciting for them but proved to be a *mixed blessing* for SMI. One such story concerns Jim Mize who was a distributor in Georgia. After several years of success in his business, Mize came to

Waco to be a part of the home office executive staff. His work here was just as outstanding as his earlier performance as a distributor, and he seemed quite satisfied with his career. But one morning he walked dejectedly into Paul's office and sat down. "Something has happened that I don't know how to handle," he began. Jim assured Paul that he was completely happy in his SMI position, but an unexpected opportunity had come his way that he felt he could not refuse.

A client who had purchased SMI programs for the people in his new car dealership and had also become a close friend had called Mize a day or two earlier to report the continued growth and success of his business—growth so pronounced that he now needed a partner to help manage the business. Because of his gratitude for the help Mize had given him, he offered Jim a gift of half interest in the business if he would come and help in the management—a gift worth in excess of $1,000,000.00. Jim was worried that Paul would think he was going back on his commitment to SMI, and he could not be happy if that were true. His joy was unbounded when Paul jumped up, grabbed his hand, and said, "Of course, you'll take it. You can't afford to miss such an opportunity." So SMI lost an outstanding producer as Jim Mize moved on to achieve his personal dreams.

Another valued team member whose personal dreams led him away from SMI was Chuck Curione. Chuck was one of the top Distributors in the LMI Division, especially effective in selling LMI programs to companies in his home city in California. He had joined LMI after retiring from a career as a United States Naval officer. After some time as a leading distributor, he was invited to move into the home office as a sales executive. His performance was marked by excellence in every area. As he continued to use his SMI program and work in his *Plan of Action,* Chuck revived a dream of many years' standing. From his youth Chuck had wanted to be a lawyer, but various circumstances had kept him out of law school, and he had pushed that desire into the background of his subconscious mind. Now he was middle aged. One day he awoke to the realization that his dream still exerted a tremendous pull for him—and he was definitely getting no younger. He explained to Paul Meyer, "This goal setting really works. I hate to leave LMI because I love it and the people. But this whole atmosphere has stirred up my dream and I have to go for it." He applied to Baylor University Law School and was admitted. Of course, that meant leaving his home office position.

To finance his education, Chuck reactivated his SMI Distributorship in a city in west Texas. During the week, he lived in Waco and studied law. On week ends, he flew to west Texas and sold SMI programs. Both his studies and his sales activities were an outstanding success. He continued weekend commuting until he had completed his law degree and passed the Texas Bar exams. For more than a decade now, he has been a highly successful lawyer in one of the largest cities in Texas.

The SMI business has always attracted people who, because they were already successful, recognized the intrinsic value of the programs and the impact they could make on the lives of all kinds of people. One such person was Ike Morrison. Born and reared on a cotton plantation in northeast Texas, Ike learned about management by working as a straw boss for his father. At the age of sixteen, Ike collected scrap iron and sold it for $6.75. He used $5.00 from the sale as a *grubstake* and bought a calf. By the age of thirty-five, he had multiplied that single calf into three thousand acres of land and four hundred head of brood cows—in spite of taking out four years to serve in the Air Force and another four years to earn a degree in agricultural education from Texas A & M. He then turned to selling agricultural products and found his true calling—professional selling. In 1960 Ike heard about the infant company, SMI, and came by to take a look. He visited with Paul Meyer to ask just what made him tick. Paul told him about the *Million Dollar Personal Success Plan* and his dream to "motivate people to their full potential." Ike shared with Paul his own philosophy for achievement—the four D's: direction, desire, determination and dedication. An immediate rapport developed between the two, and Ike Morrison became the second SMI Distributor.

For the next five years, Ike Morrison played a key role in the growth and development of SMI. Without a doubt, he was the best group seller ever associated with the company. He traveled all over the United States selling programs to hundreds of groups—large and small. One morning Ike came into Paul's office and said he had to tell Paul what was going on in his life. He explained that his association with SMI had scraped off some of his old negative thought patterns, cranked up his dream machine, and activated a dormant desire—one he had always considered to be just an idle wish that could never be transformed into reality: he wanted to build homes for underprivileged boys and girls. He even had a name for them—Boys' Country and

Girls' Country. He had decided that all of his time must go into that project.

Ike and his wife Annie Ruth moved to Houston and Ike began to talk with people about investing in his dream. One man agreed to help—with a gift of twenty-five dollars; but Ike was so persistent in presenting the need that his prospect caught a glimpse of Ike's dream and embraced it as his own. Over the next few years, he invested $2,000,000.00 in the project. When Boys' Country was well under way, a real estate developer asked Ike to help him sell some homes. Since Ike had a little more free time on his hands, he agreed to train some salespeople. In a short time, Ike Morrison had become the top deluxe home sales specialist in America, with sixty salespeople in his organization. In 1983, his company's sales topped $120,000,000.00. His goal for the balance of the 1980's involves some subdivision projects that will bring into the company a billion dollars in sales. Ike's business success has not dimmed his vision of his major dream: Boys' Country and Girls' Country are both thriving communities, providing homes and Christian values for youth who would otherwise be thrown onto the streets to fend for themselves. Ike is an outstanding example of an SMI Distributor who thoroughly embraced the concepts of the programs, became a true "product of the product," and developed a plan of action to achieve his own fantastic dreams.

Everywhere Paul Meyer goes he sees people whom he *knows* are just right for careers in SMI. (Sometimes it appears he believes SMI is the ideal career for everyone!) In 1963, Paul made a trip to Australia because someone was attempting to market copies of SMI programs and to obtain ownership of trademarks that were used on SMI products. He finally completed the business—successfully, of course—and found himself with several hours to spare before catching a plane back to the United States. He stepped out of lobby of his hotel and stood there thinking about how he could best use that time to see something of the beautiful city of Melbourne before going to the airport. He saw a young man standing on the sidewalk and offered to give him twenty dollars to provide a quick tour of the city. The young man, whose name was Graham McDougal, agreed.

In that short time of sightseeing, Paul and Graham became good friends. Paul asked Graham to describe his most important dream. Graham knew immediately! He wanted to come to the United States, but he could not come without a sponsor, and he knew no one who would qualify. Paul offered to be his sponsor, and arrangements were quickly concluded for Graham and his wife to come to Texas. Paul met the plane in Dallas and helped the young couple find a place to live. Graham began working as a distributor for SMI in the Dallas area and was soon enjoying a thriving business. He frequently attended the training schools in Waco and maintained his personal contact with Meyer. While he was building his business, Graham was busy trying to make arrangements to be granted status as a permanent resident of the United States. But that was not to be possible. Finally, he accepted the fact that he must go back to Australia. He wanted to continue as an SMI distributor in Australia, but at that time SMI products were subject to such high import duties in Australia that marketing was not feasible. In true SMI spirit, however, Graham transferred his SMI experience into another business. He started a cosmetics firm in Australia. He set goals, built a sound management and sales team, and promptly became a success. In five years he sold his company to Mary Kay Cosmetics for one million dollars.

One of the basic principles of goal setting that Paul Meyer includes in every SMI program is the necessity for crystallizing your thinking about the goals that are top priority for you. Many people become SMI distributors just because they see the company as an excellent business opportunity. Once they begin actively using their own SMI programs, they either discover for the first time what dream actually belongs at the top of their priority list, or they find the courage and self-confidence to believe that they can achieve a dream that has seemed too far above them in the past. Meyer looks at the *turnover* figures caused when these people leave SMI as positive indicators that the programs work.

Brian Popko is an example of a distributor who found SMI a means of both personal growth and career expansion. Brian joined SMI in the 1960's and quickly became one of the most productive members of the distributorship organization. He began to specialize in selling programs to companies for use by groups of managers. This approach made it possible to market a much larger volume of programs than he could have sold through one-on-one personal sales. In 1976, Popko closed the largest single sale of SMI programs on record: $103,000.00. Popko eventually moved on to pursuit of his own dream: the Millionaire's Club, an exclusive club for upscale singles. His organization now has eight metropolitan locations. The club provides RSVP parties, high-tech pairing, travel programs, and personal development seminars. The clubs also sponsor retirement plans. His next project is a magazine for singles. Brian is still a strong supporter of SMI and a real center of influence for Meyer. Paul, in turn, follows Popko's success with interest. "There are," Paul declares, "no golden handcuffs in SMI. People are free to reach for their own stars."

CHAPTER EIGHT
RELATIONSHIPS

Opportunity
is not
what may come
tomorrow,

but

what we make of
today!

Paul J. Meyer

CHAPTER EIGHT

RELATIONSHIPS

REACHING OUT

The beliefs and attitudes that have gone into the personal make-up of Paul Meyer are evidenced in the kind of relationships he maintains with people in every area of his life. Both his mother's open love and trust in all people and his father's inability to express his emotional commitment to others have deeply affected him. As did his mother, Paul believes that all people have depths of innate worth and potential that they can call upon if they are challenged to do so. From her he also learned that the worth and potential of people are most likely to surface when the environment is one of encouragement, love, and acceptance. Even in his youth, Paul recognized his father's wordless yearning for the ability to establish and maintain open, loving relationships with others; and he early decided that building relationships of friendship and love with many was a goal so important that he would allow nothing to rob him of the happiness that loving relationships provide. He has never counted it too risky to leave himself vulnerable in the pursuit of personal relationships.

Allowing himself to be vulnerable has occasionally resulted in Paul's suffering hurt. For example, in 1970, SMI was doing very well. The company was growing, and many of the early problems had been solved. At that time, SMI, as well as a number of the people in the company, were doing business with a relatively new bank whose offices were near SMI's. Out of the clear blue one day, the president of the bank telephoned thirty-eight people who were officers and managers in SMI to tell them that their loans—car loans, home loans, and personal loans—were being called immediately. He then called Paul and told him that SMI's loan was also being called. The total amount was almost two million dollars. There was no way the company and all thirty-eight of those people could raise that money overnight. Paul took them all down to another, older bank in town and asked that bank to cover all those loans. The bank agreed to do so on the condition that Paul cosign all the notes and put up his company as collateral. They further agreed to give make all the notes for five years. But two years later, the bank president got worried about so much money loaned to people in one company and called the loans again.

By that time, a number of the thirty-eight people whose notes Paul had signed had left the company. A few of them had paid their notes, but quite a few of them had fallen behind in the debts they left in Waco. When the notes were called, it was Meyer who would have to pay. He sold land and real estate and borrowed from still another bank to meet the demand. He was desperate to raise the money because the collateral was the controlling stock in SMI, and he did not want to lose control of the company. Paul eventually paid off all the loans, as he had paid off the losses of the insurance company some years before. Again his trust in people and his willingness to risk hurt in search of close relationships had brought him close to disaster. But the experience did not change his belief in the innate worth and goodness of people, and he still reaches out to others.

The climate in a corporation almost always reflects the personality and value system of its founder. SMI is no exception. People are *expected* to achieve, to succeed—not under threat of punishment, but from a positive belief in their potential. The result has been the formation of a team of officers and executives who accept responsibility for their individual duties, work hard to meet their goals and support one another because they feel a sense of comradeship and personal commitment to each other and to the company. Paul finds among the company officers and executives some of his closest friends. He enjoys family get-togethers with some, tennis matches with others, and group social events with all. When people speak of the "SMI family," that phrase has real significance. Coworkers feel a sense of kinship; they rejoice in one another's victories, and support and comfort those who face problems or difficulties. The stories told by various SMI officers illustrate Paul's willingness to believe in human potential. Their backgrounds, the levels of success they had reached before joining SMI, and the paths they have followed to achievement in the company show little in common except that Paul Meyer believed in them, expected success, and then stepped back and allowed them to work out their own personal destinies.

THE HOME OFFICE FAMILY

A prime example of one who has succeeded largely as a result of the trust placed in him by Meyer is James L. Sirbasku, who is now president of SMI International, Inc., the parent holding company of the marketing divisions. Jim first joined SMI as a distributor. His prior work experience consisted of eight years as a meat cutter in a packing plant, the same job held by his father for forty years and his grandfather for another forty before him; but Jim wanted something more from life. Having learned about SMI through an ad in a magazine, Jim came to Waco, with his wife Judy, to be interviewed as a distributor prospect. No one thought he had much potential for success in the business—no one, that is, except Paul Meyer. Jim was allowed to become a distributor almost solely on the basis of Paul's insistence on the policy of refusing to prejudge anyone's ability to succeed.

From the very first day of his association with SMI, Jim Sirbasku looked to Paul Meyer as a role model and a mentor. At the time Jim became a distributor, SMI's corporate structure was still relatively simple; there was only Success Motivation Institute, Inc., with several departments that would later become separate subsidiary companies. Paul was the president of the company, and was actively involved in distributor recruitment and training as well as in corporate management. Just a few months after becoming a distributor, Jim attended a training school in Waco and heard Paul speak. At the end of the session, Jim made his way through the crowd to shake hands with Paul. So caught up was he in the emotional impact of the moment that Jim had no idea what he would say to Paul. He only knew he wanted to touch him and speak to him. In one of those "twilight zone" experiences, Jim heard himself saying, "Paul, some day I am going to be the President of SMI." Immediately, he was appalled. Why did he say that? Would Paul feel insulted that this green distributor had the nerve to state his intention to take over Paul's job? Had Jim ruined his chances for any future advancement? Paul's reaction was typical. "I believe you can," he said. "It's up to you."

Jim Sirbasku took Paul's reply seriously. He knew the first step was to be successful as a distributor. He worked incredibly hard; he fol-

The most successful leaders are those who recognize the creative potential of everyone on their team and make productive use of it.

Paul J. Meyer

lowed all the training materials meticulously; he sought the guidance of his sales director and followed his suggestions; he recruited and trained a large sales organization. Then after three years as a distributor, Jim was asked to come to Waco to be interviewed for a position as a sales director. Paul expressed his confidence that Jim could succeed in this endeavor just as he had succeeded as a distributor. Later when he was asked to accept appointment as Director of Training for the company, it was again Paul's encouragement that gave Jim the courage to move out in another new direction. When Paul recommended that Jim be promoted to vice-president of one of the sales divisions, every member of the Board of Directors voted against the decision—everyone, that is, except Paul Meyer. Paul insisted that Jim could do the job; his judgment prevailed, and Jim was promoted. A few years later, Jim was made president of Success Motivation Institute, Inc., and then also of Leadership Management, Inc. In 1983, Paul stepped aside as president of SMI International, Inc., the parent holding company of both Success Motivation Institute, Inc., and Leadership Management, Inc., retaining his position as Chairman of the Board. By that time, it was obvious that Jim Sirbasku was the logical choice for the position of president.

Jim Sirbasku gives credit to Paul's programs for the growth he has experienced personally and professionally. He still listens regularly to SMI programs for their positive impact on all six areas of his life and their ability to enhance his self-image, to provide a positive direction for goals, and to create a positive mental attitude. When he came to the home office, Jim consciously took Paul as an example in social situations, in management action, and in attitudes. Jim believes that he has been able to grow in his professional life and as a human being largely because Paul believed in him. He sees his association with SMI as a vehicle that has enabled him to express his personal values and beliefs, to grow in all areas of life, to serve people, and to become financially independent.

Ferrell Hunter, administrative vice-president of SMI International, Inc., has a career background about as diverse as one person could amass—all in one company. After college, Ferrell served in the armed forces for several years. When his enlistment was up, he went to work for SMI. The company was just getting started, and Ferrell was assigned to the shipping department, packing boxes at a salary of $2.50 per hour. Paul was interested in Ferrell and urged him to believe in himself, to discover the real potential he had available for use. As

Ferrell mastered one job, Paul moved him up to something more challenging. Over the more than twenty years of his SMI career, Ferrell has been involved in almost every facet of the business: actual selling in the field, sales training for distributors, helping to develop sales training manuals and sales promotion materials, recruiting new distributors, and administrative trouble shooting of all kinds. For a period of several years, he was senior vice president of the Leadership Management, Inc., sales division. In his present position, he has—among other duties—helped to set up a computer system for the marketing divisions, working with the systems people to determine the kinds of records and reports needed for efficient management.

Like many others, Ferrell remembers a "little" experience that represents for him the impact of Paul's influence on his life. It happened when Ferrell was about twenty-five. "In my early teens I had grown quickly," Ferrell remembers, "and was clumsy. I learned how to cover up the clumsiness when I was in the eighth or ninth grade by joking it off and apologizing for it. I didn't realize that every time I joked about it or apologized for it, I kept the clumsiness alive. One evening my wife and I were having dinner at Paul's and I turned over a glass of iced tea. I jumped up to clean up the mess and started joking about my clumsiness. Paul said, 'I don't care if you tear my house down—but don't ever again apologize or recognize in any way the fact that you are clumsy where I can hear it.' I thought he was being harsh, but the advice worked. When I quit mentally recognizing and affirming my clumsiness, most of it disappeared."

Because he came to SMI with no prior business experience, Ferrell has gained all of his professional expertise in the company. He has developed outstanding sales and management skills as well as the ability to earn, manage, and invest his own income. But SMI programs and concepts have worked for him in other areas of life, too. He tells it like this: "Probably the greatest thing I learned from SMI was how to use the principles taught in the programs to be a better parent. Since my dad died when I was very young and my family soon disintegrated, I had no role models for being a parent. I had to learn it all. My association with SMI taught me how to feed my children positive affirmations, how to help them set goals, how to help them prize their own uniqueness and use it, how to accept them as they are, and how to help them build confidence."

Rex Houze, executive vice-president of Leadership Management, Inc., a division of SMI International, Inc., is an example of one who came to the SMI family already a professional success. He was employed by the state in civil engineering—heavy construction and highway—working with the design and building of bridges and highways. Even then, however, Rex was interested in working with people to help them use their potential. He pursued this interest through active involvement in the Jaycees. He served as state president of this organization that consisted of over three hundred chapters and fifteen thousand members in his state.

In 1972, Rex decided to become a distributor in the LMI division of the company. His engineering background can be seen in the orderly, purposeful way he went about building his business. His interest in people was expressed as he recruited an active sales organization and led them to win consistent recognition for achievement. His rapid advancement caught the attention of Paul and other company officials, and he was invited to join the home office staff as a sales director; later he was made vice-president of sales, and then executive vice-president.

After fifteen years in the company, Rex Houze still listens daily to Paul's program, the *Dynamics of Personal Leadership,* and feels that its ideas and inspiration have permeated his life in every area. He also listens frequently to tapes of Paul's speeches to the sales organization for direct application of program ideas to the operation of the business. Rex lists three principles that he has learned from his association with Paul and through using the program:

> "Personal responsibility: if it is to be, it's up to me.
>
> Initiative: the ability to be a self-starter.
>
> Self-reliance: the ability to get the job done without being told what to do."

It is interesting to note that Rex describes these principles as the ones "that have helped me most and that I will try to perpetuate with my children." Even though Paul does not attempt to direct or even to suggest what people in the company should do in their families, it is in their families that people most often experience the greatest satisfaction when they seek to internalize the ideas presented in Paul's writings. Of the three principles that he lists as having impressed him, Rex Houze says, "I have seen Paul Meyer exemplify these three concepts as a businessman, family man, tennis player and as a friend."

SMI's resident home-office sports expert is Buddy Haney, the president of Success Motivation Institute, Inc., one of the marketing divisions of SMI International, Inc. After college, Buddy played center field for the Kansas City (now Los Angeles) Athletics for several seasons, spent some time as a baseball coach, and then went to work in a family-owned heating and air conditioning business. But he still had the spirit of a competitor and the love of helping other people achieve that had marked his work as a coach. In the early 1970's he decided that someone else in the family could run the heating and air conditioning business, and he became a distributor for SMI. In a short time, his hard work and drive to achieve moved him up into the ranks of the top performers in his division, and he was asked to come into the home office as a sales executive. His will to win continued to push him to high achievement, and he was a consistent high achiever. In 1984, he was promoted to his current position, president of Success Motivation Institute, Inc.

Just a few months after Buddy Haney joined the home office staff, he was sitting in his office one evening making telephone calls to prospective distributors. But the calls just did not seem to be accomplishing much. As he hung up the receiver after another discouraging call, he heard a voice from his office door say, "Nice guys don't win—they don't even place." Buddy turned around to see Paul Meyer standing there. Buddy must have looked puzzled, for Paul went on to explain that it is all well and good to be "nice" and "polite," but if that keeps you from asking questions, from challenging a prospect's statement that he "can't afford it," or from discovering just what the prospect *does* need, then you haven't really been "nice." Actually, you have failed to serve the prospect—and you have lost the chance to make a sale that will benefit both you and the prospect. The lesson lasted less than three minutes, but Buddy is still benefiting from its impact. The next day, Buddy remembered that Paul had written an article with the title *Nice Guys Don't Win* for distribution to the sales organization. He had seen it, but now it had real meaning for him. He got a copy and studied it over and over. Today Buddy Haney is a "nice" guy, but not the kind of namby-pamby nice guy who takes "no" for an answer from someone who should be saying "yes."

Like so many other SMI people, Buddy thinks of his family when he lists the benefits he has enjoyed from his association with SMI and Meyer. In addition to helping him grow personally and become a well-rounded person, SMI concepts have helped him rear his three sons.

All of his boys have used SMI programs and have become fine young men and outstanding athletes. The older two have already earned full scholarships to play in Southwest Conference colleges.

L.D. Tanner is an interesting member of the home office staff. As a young man serving in the U.S. Navy, he made up his mind that he would pursue a career in consumer finance. He first became interested in the field when he consented to cosign a note for a friend and was impressed with the professionalism and integrity of the financial institution that handled the transaction. While in the Navy he had the opportunity to study at the University of the Philippines. After his enlistment was up, he secured a position with a reputable firm and began to study and train himself for a career in the business. He graduated from the Cornell University Advanced Management Course in Business Administration and received specialized training in all phases of consumer finance. When he first heard of SMI, he had advanced to the position of senior regional manager for the western region of a major nation-wide financial institution.

Tanner first met Paul Meyer when Meyer came to New York to explore sources of consumer financing that would be available to SMI distributors for their clients. A large bank in New York referred Paul to the company for which Tanner worked, and Tanner was sent to Texas to explore the possibility of setting up the needed finance system. He quickly set up a pilot program for the distributors in Texas, then added California and finally Canada. He went back to New York, never expecting to have any further contact with SMI or Waco, Texas. But in 1971, Paul and the SMI Board of Directors were ready to establish their own consumer financing company to serve distributors. Who, they asked, was better qualified to to do the job than L.D. Tanner. So they asked him to leave his assured career path to start a new company from scratch. L.D. surprised himself by accepting the offer. "It was a combination of factors that helped me decide to come," L.D. remembers. "I liked Paul Meyer and the SMI officers. I liked the company and what they were doing. And it was a real challenge to build a finance company entirely on my own—to have an opportunity to install all of my own system, principles and procedures, and to prove that I could do it."

Tanner remembers that all of his colleagues in New York warned him that moving to Waco, Texas, was a sure path to failure and oblivion. They didn't believe anyone could pull off the job Meyer described. "The finance business often makes people prone to negative attitudes," L.D. says, "but here at SMI you lose a lot of that attitude. You begin to believe—and then you are free to succeed." L.D. sees his association with Paul Meyer and SMI as one of the best things that ever happened to him. He is wealthier, healthier, and happier than he ever expected to be. "Paul has even changed my eating habits," he laughs. "But most of all, he is my friend."

Joe Baxter, President of Success Motivation International, Inc., joined SMI as Comptroller when the company was less than three years old. Prior to his association with SMI, Joe had been the business manager of a large Waco church and later was general manager of an oil company. As the company grew, Joe's responsibilities also grew. He was soon made Secretary-Treasurer of the corporation, and in the late 1970's he was appointed Vice-President, and later President of SMI's international division.

Since assuming leadership of the international marketing, Joe has traveled to seventy countries all over the free world to recruit new distributors and to work with those already active in the business. He is in constant touch by telephone and facsimile mail with the worldwide organization. In all of these contacts Joe has been most impressed with the similarities of people in widely separated countries and cultures that are seemingly quite unrelated. He has found that no matter how different their cultures and customs might be, people all over the world have common desires for success, shared aspirations for personal improvement, and similar needs for achievement. Because of their shared needs and their similar natures, people all over the world respond to SMI programs that speak to their aspirations. Helping people to discover how they can use more of their talents and abilities for the success they desire has made Baxter's job an exciting and rewarding one.

SMI International's senior vice president, Charles (Chuck) Williams, has been with the company since 1965. Chuck first met Paul in 1963 when he was assigned by the accounting firm where he was a CPA to do a special tax planning project for SMI. He was impressed with Paul Meyer, his dream, and the SMI products. As a result, he set a goal to become the financial vice president of SMI. In less than a year, Paul asked Chuck if he would consider becoming an officer of the young company. Chuck shared with Paul the goal he had set some months earlier and outlined the type of position he felt he could fill effectively.

During the twenty years Chuck has been an officer and member of the Board of Directors, he and Paul have developed a close working relationship based on mutual loyalty. The qualities that originally attracted Chuck to Paul and to SMI have been confirmed and expanded as their relationship developed. "I have never been forced to become a 'yes man' in order to do my job," Chuck reflects. "Paul expects a great deal from people, but he always leaves them free to express their opinions and beliefs. He allows them the freedom to be themselves while they are working out the job he has assigned to them."

Just a few months after Chuck joined the company, Paul asked him to take over a special project. Two other people had already attempted it, but neither had succeeded. Chuck went back to his office and thought about it for several hours. Then he made a list of the problems and obstacles that would have to be overcome before the project could be completed. He went back to Paul and showed him the list. Paul agreed that Chuck's list was probably accurate. Then he asked Chuck to list ten approaches that could be used to achieve the desired result and to prioritize them according to their probability of success. When Chuck returned with the list, Paul complimented him on his creative thinking and then told him to implement the *tenth* option—not the first. "I learned," Chuck remembers, "that it is possible to overcome obstacles and to achieve goals even through the least desirable means. Success is always possible for one who is determined to achieve it."

The president of Leadership Management, Inc., one of the sales divisions of SMI International, Inc., is John Appel. John was working in a family dry cleaning business when he first heard of SMI from a brother-in-law, a pilot for a major airlines, who had been using an SMI program. John purchased a program for himself and began using it in his own personal life and also in his business. He liked the program so much that he contacted SMI and ultimately became a distributor in his home town in Iowa. After two years, in 1971, he was asked to come to the home office as a Development Director. He was soon made Vice President for Development, and later Vice President of Success Motivation Institute, Inc. Several years—and several promotions—later he was made president of the LMI division.

Appel is a strong supporter of Paul Meyer and SMI. He points to his financial independence as the most tangible evidence of how SMI

Building Success Attitudes

Eliminate these words completely	Add these words to your vocabulary
1. I can't	I can
2. If	I will
3. Doubt	Expect the best
4. I don't think	I know
5. I don't have time	I will make the time
6. Maybe	Positively
7. I'm afraid	I am confident
8. I don't believe	I do believe
9. Minimize "I"	Promote "You"

Paul J. Meyer

has benefited his life; but he is quick to say money is the least important facet of his business experience. He considers the opportunity to help other people achieve their potential and to succeed in life to be the most rewarding part of his career with SMI. Personally, he credits Paul Meyer's programs with giving him an awareness of his potential to grow and the knowledge of what he can become. Working in the various positions he has filled has given John the ability to maintain a positive attitude in times of adversity, to believe in his ability to overcome problems, and to cope with adverse circumstances and solve problems. He is attempting to pass on to his children the importance of adopting a goal-directed attitude toward life.

Paul Meyer's interest and attention is not limited to the officers and executives of the company. He is just as concerned for the needs and achievements of secretaries, technicians, clerical workers and manufacturing people. Several years ago, for example, one of the sales directors reported to Paul that his secretary had to have serious spinal surgery. Her doctor had said she would be unable to work for a year. Company insurance would pay most of her medical costs, but sick leave would be exhausted months before she could return to work. The problem was that she was the sole support of herself and a young child. Paul turned to his dictating machine and recorded a memo to the personnel department instructing them to pay the secretary's full salary for a year and to see that she had a job when she was ready to return to work. The young woman was dumbfounded. She came to see Paul to express her gratitude and asked why he was willing to do this for her when he had never even met her except to see her in the hallway. "I did it because you are important to our company," Paul said. "You and the other employees are as much a part of SMI as I am. What affects you, affects all of us. That's why we have health insurance for all our people. In your case, it isn't enough. We are just supplementing the insurance so you can get well."

This was not an isolated instance. Other needs have been met as well, and employees often participate personally in helping one another with special needs such as severe or prolonged illness. One long-time employee took an extended leave of absence when her husband had a heart transplant. He recovered and lived several additional years. Although she had returned to work, his illness and death left the wife with huge bills to pay. SMI gave her a large bonus—an amount that went a long way toward relieving her of the pressing debt; and coworkers added their own contributions. But it is not just finan-

Billy and Deborah Meyer and their children, Christen and Adam.

Jim and Ann Meyer and sons Brady and Mike.

cial hardship that prompts special attention from the company. A secretary in the company had a goal to make a trip to Washington, D.C., to see the monument to service personnel killed in the Vietnam conflict—one of whom was her son. She expected to take several years to save enough money to make the trip. Paul found out about her goal, and the company gave her travel money so she could make the trip without the long wait.

In addition to the hard work they put into their careers, all of the officers as well as many of the employees at all levels in the various SMI family of companies are also active in church and civic work. Several of the officers serve in various capacities in the Waco Boys' Club and the Central Texas Council of the Boy Scouts of America, and in the civic clubs in the Waco area.

Perhaps one company practice illustrates better than anything else the spirit of family togetherness that exists: the company telephone directory is alphabetized by *first names*—for officers, clerical workers and manufacturing employees.

THE MEYER FAMILY

In spite of his drive for business success and the long hours he gives to work, Paul Meyer has always found time for his family. Every SMI program includes a section on family life goals in the *Plan of Action*. It is Paul's firm belief that building satisfying family relationships is one of the chief purposes for a personal goals program. Success in a career or business makes possible the financial structure for supporting and caring for the family. Developing positive attitudes and habits aids one in giving children a firm foundation for a satisfying and successful life. The memories and experiences of the Meyer children provide some interesting insights into the kind of person Paul has become and the values he considers most important.

Paul's oldest son, Jim, remembers a chart that hung on the wall in the play room even before he knew how to read. It was titled *Building Success Attitudes,* and it listed a number of words that should be eliminated from the vocabulary along with some words to replace them. Paul frequently called attention to the chart and urged the children to say "I can" instead of "I can't," and "I will" rather than "I won't." Jim remembers that "about the only time he was ever upset with us was when we said we couldn't do something. He told us to

Jim Meyer
Balance Sheet
March 13, 1971

Assets

Current Assets	
Cash in bank	$ 75
Marketable securities, at market	3,927
Automobile	5,000
Other personal property	3,000
	12,002
Intangible Assets	
Intelligent	
Appreciative	
Sincere	
Competitive	
Responsible	
Aggressive	1,063,931
Persistent	
Aesthetic	
God-Fearing	
Enthusiastic	
Tolerant	
Cooperative	
Courteous	
Ambitious	
Healthy	
	1,063,931
Other Assets	
Jim Meyer Trust— net equity at market	420,261
Cash value life insurance	3,806
	$1,500,000

Liabilities and Net Worth

Total Liabilities (See Note)	$ 0
Jim Meyer—Net Worth	1,500,000
	$1,500,000

Note – Because of the above Intangible Assets possessed by Jim Meyer, and our knowledge and belief that he will continue to nurture and develop these assets, we feel that this young man has no liabilities that will materially affect him or his future.

finish what we started. I think that's what enabled me to get through law school in spite of the many times I would have liked to quit. I know that's why I completed pilot's training and got my flying license although I knew thirty hours into the training that I didn't want to be a pilot. I just never thought of quitting."

His father's attitudes evidently took root early in Jim's thinking. When he was about nine or ten years old, Jim wrote a little book—several handwritten pages—which he called *Only He Can Who Thinks He Can.* Jim evidently thinks he can. He has achieved outstanding success as an attorney for one as young as he is. He has earned certification by the State Bar of Texas as a specialist in both family law and criminal trial law and is recognized in the Central Texas area as an excellent trial lawyer. Jim sees trying cases as closely akin to his father's professional sales activity. He uses many of the same persuasive skills salespeople use as he attempts to "sell" his client, his case, and his ideas to the jury.

When Jim's twenty-first birthday came, Paul began a tradition that has become standard family practice in the Meyer household. Up until that age, Paul provides each child a minimum allowance (although he expects each one to do specific work appropriate to age and abilities), pays for whatever educational pursuits each one chooses, and generally supports and teaches each one to be independent and productive. Jim's birthday present was an official-looking financial document headed "Jim Meyer, Balance Sheet." It listed the personal qualities Jim possessed as intangible assets—intelligent, responsible, God-fearing, and enthusiastic. A monetary value was assigned to each of these assets. Under liabilities, a note stated that Jim had no liabilities that would materially affect him. His *net worth* was shown at $1,500,000.00. A note from Paul was attached expressing love for Jim, confidence that he would be a winner throughout his adult life, as he had been as a child and a youth—and the final expression of Paul's "confidence"—the news that Jim was now on his own.

When asked what made him choose law as a career, Jim laughs and says, "I didn't want to work at SMI." He had worked part time in various jobs in the company during his student days, and he had observed that everyone just assumed he would automatically have an executive position in SMI when he finished school. But he didn't want to succeed as the *boss's son.* He wanted success on his own account—not because his father paved the way for him. The personal balance sheet he received for his birthday was evidently accurate in describing him as "ambitious, competitive," and "persistent." Paul had always told him he could do anything he wanted to do—and Jim believed it. So he set out to succeed by using his potential with the positive attitudes he had learned from his father.

Like Paul, Jim has always enjoyed sports. "Dad was always competitive," Jim recalls, "and it was important to win. But it was also important to be a good sport. If we played the game and lost, he was upset *only* if we were bad sports. He taught us that it was ok to lose if you used the experience to learn something. He would sit down and say, 'So you lost. How will you change next time? Do you know where you were weak? What did you do wrong? What did you fail to do that you could have done? What do you need to practice before the next game?' Then he would help us make a plan of action to correct any problem before the next time."

Jim has used that same approach in coaching a soccer team for boys. His team recently lost a game for the first time in two years. At the next practice, he had the boys sit down and together they made a list of things they could do better and how they would practice those things before the next game. His players still regard themselves as winners—and they are because they learned from this temporary setback. They will be better players and better people as a result.

"Dad never shoved SMI courses down our throats," Jim recalls. "Actually, I don't think he even knows whether we have ever listened to one of his programs or not. I guess he thought it wasn't important. We have lived those concepts all our lives, and they are imprinted on our minds and personalities. We have learned a lot more from his attitudes and example than we would ever have learned from reading the programs or listening to tapes." Jim and his wife Anne are attempting to use the same approach to rearing their sons that Paul used with his children. Brady and Mike, now eleven and nine years of age, both have a large dose of the Meyer competitive spirit and thirst for success. Both excellent athletes, they are members of soccer teams that have won state-wide tournaments in their respective age groups. They are also both good at basketball, baseball, and tennis. Jim and his boys are listening together to one of Paul's courses, *The Making of a Champion*, a program of goal setting and achievement attitudes for young athletes. Jim follows Paul's practice of helping his boys dream of lofty goals, work for their achievement, and maintain a positive attitude toward all that is required in the process. On the wall in the play room of his home is a large chart entitled, *Building Success Attitudes*.

Larry, Paul's second son, enjoyed a birthday gift from his father similar to that Jim received. When his twenty-first birthday came, Larry was in college. Early the morning of that day he received a large birthday card from his father. Across the bottom was written "Welcome to the free enterprise system, Love, Dad." Larry turned it over, read it again, and then picked up the phone and called Paul. "Dad, what do you mean, 'Welcome to the free enterprise system'?" Paul's reply was typical: "I mean just what I say: welcome to the real world—the world where everyone is responsible for himself, his achievement and his success. You've had your last allowance check."

Larry had evidently been so absorbed in his own interests when Jim received his "present" that it hadn't soaked in that he might be getting one like it. At first he was somewhat at a loss; so he asked Paul what he should do. Paul countered with a question: "What do you *want* to do?" Larry knew! He wanted to be a part of SMI. For the first time in Larry's memory, Paul was not encouraging. He refused to help. "I'm not going to cripple you by doing things for you that you should do for yourself," was Paul's reasoning. He would not give or buy Larry an SMI distributorship, he wouldn't even loan him the money to buy one, and he refused to give him any kind of job in the home office although for several years Larry, like Jim, had worked in the company during school vacations. In typical Meyer fashion, Larry decided to do it for himself.

While trying to figure out the best way to "do it for himself," Larry attended an annual SMI convention in Canada, visited with Ted Kemper, head of SMI's Canadian company, and took a look at the way the company operated there. Ted was encouraging. He told Larry he believed he could succeed as an SMI distributor. On the way home, Larry visited Mike Hawkins, a dynamic young SMI distributor. He followed Mike around for several days, watching him make sales presentations to prospects and to prospective sales recruits. Mike was encouraging, as Kemper had been, and Larry thought he could do what Mike was doing. Larry also stopped by to visit Joe Charbonneau, one of the leading distributors in the company at that time, and gained another friend who told Larry that he had real potential for success in SMI. Back at home, Larry set out to complete his homework. He researched ten different cities where he might establish his business.

Larry and Lynn Meyer and daughter Jessica.

Paul Meyer, the grandfather, with Mike and Brady Meyer.

Finally, he chose Houston, Texas, one of the fastest-growing cities in the nation. It had the added advantage of being near enough to Waco so that he could attend training meetings frequently. His choice made, Larry contacted SMI's home office and made arrangements to attend the development cycle offered to all those who consider SMI as a career. He listened to the presentation of the business opportunity and indicated his desire to become a distributor. He was accepted and arranged his own financing to purchase the franchise.

Paul purposely avoided discussing business with Larry. He refused to give him any coaching or suggestions that would seem to give him any preferment over other distributors. He knew that Larry must succeed on his own or any recognition he received would do him more harm than good. He told all the officers of the company that Larry was to be treated exactly as any other distributor. That is how Larry's favorite story evolved. Just a few months after launching his company, Larry made a large company sale. He had on hand only a portion of the inventory he needed to make delivery. He needed an additional $2,000.00 worth of programs, but he didn't have the cash.

As soon as he could deliver the programs, he would have a check for $7,000.00 from the company and could pay for the inventory. He called his sales director, Bill Cochran, and placed the order. Then Larry told Bill that he didn't have the cash, and the bank had refused to loan him any more—but he could pay for the programs the day after he delivered them. "Well," Bill said, "I'll have to get permission to give you credit. You know that all merchandise is shipped only for cash. That's our policy for all distributors. The company doesn't want distributors to be hampered by debt for inventory. That just isn't good business." The answer Bill received was a firm *No*. Larry was desperate. He finally called Rose Frost, Paul's personal accountant and a long-time family friend, for advice about somewhere he might borrow $2,000.00 for a week. Rose promised to make a few inquiries and get back to him. Her "inquiry" was a request to her bank to loan her $2,000.00 on her car. She took the check to the accounting department and had Larry's order shipped. True to his promise, Larry had the money back in her hands in less than a week.

Larry recalls that Paul's action in putting him on his own and then refusing to help him start his career seemed harsh at the time. From carefree college student to businessman facing the realities of an uncaring business world was a difficult step to take. But now Larry believes Paul knew exactly what he was doing—and why. He knows that

Paul and granddaughter Jessica Meyer.

Paul and grandchildren Christen and Adam.

it was done in love, and he is grateful. At the time, he experienced some anger along with a sense of rejection. But, just as Paul knew he would, he channeled his anger into productive activity. After all, he is an inheritor of the Meyer desire for perfection, stubborn determination to achieve their goals, and wholehearted belief in their own ability to succeed. And succeed he did! It was 1971 when Larry became an SMI Distributor, and he operated his business for four years. In 1972 he was named Rookie of the Year in his sales division. In 1973, at the age of twenty-three, he was recognized as World Rookie of the Year—the best beginning distributor in the whole world-wide SMI organization. These recognitions were earned on the basis of objective criteria—sales records achieved and verified by records of inventory purchased—not by consideration of his family ties.

In 1975, Larry was invited by Jim Sirbasku to join the home office staff as a development director. His duties were to work with prospective distributors, presenting the business to them, and assisting them in the process of purchasing and setting up a franchised distributorship. He was already in the process of moving to Waco before Paul knew anything about this new development. Something of the old Meyer temper took over, and Paul stormed into Jim Sirbasku's office demanding to know why his direct orders had been disobeyed and Larry was being pushed into the home office. Jim had been expecting Paul's reaction, and he was loaded with answers. He had the records to show Larry's achievements. He had some recordings of presentations Larry had made to groups—recordings that proved his competence as a speaker and as a representative of SMI. "I need Larry on my staff," Jim continued. "After all, my job—according to you—is to meet the goals we have set for the company. To do that, I need the best staff I can get. Larry's the best; so I hired him." Paul's fatherly pride fought hard with his fear that Larry would be hampered in his career by being the boss's son. He studiously avoided any temptation to coach Larry or to help him in his work. Evidently, no such coaching was needed. Larry set top records among the development staff for four years; then he was made vice-president for development in his sales division and stayed in that position for four additional years.

While he was vice-president, Larry became interested in real estate investment. He was making an excellent income, especially for one so young, and he knew from his childhood teaching that he was responsible for investing his money and making it grow. He and Paul, along with other friends and business associates, began to form syndicates to invest in commercial real estate. While still turning in top performance in his SMI duties, Larry studied real estate diligently; he used off hours to work their "deals." One of the SMI subsidiaries is Success Properties, Inc. This company was started to invest in some commercial properties that might be used by various branches of the company or could be rented out for additional income. It was a small operation in the beginning, but at an officers' meeting one morning, Chuck Williams remarked, "Do you realize that the little bit of real estate we purchased through SPI has grown so that the assets of that company exceed the real assets of the rest of the subsidiaries? I think it is imperative that we put one of our corporate officers in charge of SPI instead of relying exclusively on operating personnel." Larry's growing interest in real estate made him ask for this position.

By April, 1983, Larry had decided to move into real estate exclusively. After a few months, he had become an independent real estate developer. In December, 1986, he capped his real estate activities by closing the largest single sale in the history of McLennan County: $29,000,000.00 in cash! This sale included a number of properties in Waco, Texas, owned by Larry, Paul, and several other partners. Some months before he completed this astounding real estate deal, Larry made another career move. He purchased T Shirts Plus, a nationwide franchise company with headquarters in Waco, Texas. He is now the president and chief executive officer of this thriving company.

Like his father, Larry is a happy family man. He and his wife Lynn have a daughter, Jessica, who was born in May, 1983. They have bought a ranch near Waco, and spend much of their family time there enjoying the outdoor life.

The third Meyer son, Billy, inherited a great deal of his father's entrepreneurial spirit. Like his brothers, he has chosen his own career path and has pursued it diligently on his own. Almost from the time he could walk, Billy has been interested in wheels—especially if they go fast. Paul allowed him to learn about all kinds of motor vehicles beginning with small dirt bikes and progressing, as he grew, to larger models, and then into cars. By the time he was old enough to drive, he was ready to move into drag racing, locally at first, but quickly moving onto the professional circuit. Billy's career choice brought Paul numerous opportunities to renounce his own parenting values. He often thought how easy it would be to tell his minor age son that racing was out—it is too dangerous! He had to remind himself many times that "success is the progressive realization of predetermined *personal* goals." *Paul's personal goals* called for protecting his children from harm—physical, emotional, and all other kinds. Unfortunately, *Billy's goals* seemed to call for putting himself in all sorts of dangerous physical situations. Paul found the answer to his dilemma by doing what he could to help Billy have safe equipment so that he had the maximum possible protection.

Billy chose the Funny Car classification in professional drag racing. Funny cars are simulated stock cars with fiber glass bodies that are replicas of American-made autos. Billy's car is modeled after the Mustang. Funny cars are powered by super charged, injected motors that run on nitromethane. For the first few years of Billy's participation on the professional racing circuit, Paul and SMI were major sponsors of his car which carried the name *SMI Motivator*. But soon that *magic* twenty-first birthday rolled around for Billy, and he received the same birthday present Jim and Larry had received before him. He was on his own. Billy reacted much as Jim and Larry had before him—first shock, then anger, then determination to succeed without his father's help. Billy told his brothers, "What's Dad's problem? Does he think I can't make it without him? I'll show him that I don't need his help!" And make it he did! He now owns his own racing team, Billy Meyer Racing, Inc., with an organization including drivers and mechanics. He owns a stable of racing cars and an eighteen-wheel semitrailer for transporting them. He is one of the consistent money-winners on the pro circuit.

One of Billy's favorite stories about his father concerns the time Paul sold Billy's golf clubs. Billy's grades had fallen below what Paul considered the acceptable level, and Paul had told him that the next semester must show significant improvement or some sort of penalty would be exacted. Billy glibly promised to do better and promptly dismissed the conversation from his mind. After all, the end of next semester was a long time off. At that particular time, Billy had become quite interested in golf and was playing almost every afternoon. One afternoon he came home from school to pick up his clubs and head for the greens. But his clubs were nowhere to be found. He couldn't imagine what had happened to them. When he told Paul about the mystery, Paul said in an off-hand manner, "Oh, I sold your clubs today. You didn't improve your grades this semester as you had promised." Billy was livid—but he got the message. Paul never had to mention grades again, and it was quite some time before Billy owned another set of golf clubs. As he looks back on that experience now, Billy

Billy Meyer's dream realized: the Motorplex.

Jane and Paul Meyer with Mike Mansfield, U.S. Ambassador to Japan, when Mansfield introduced Meyer to speak to Japan America Society, May, 1986

admits that he deserved just what happened. Furthermore, he says he will probably do the same thing, or something similar, if his own son should ever need the same kind of *reinforcement* that Paul provided for him. "It all boils down to consistency," Billy says. Paul was always predictable as a parent, and the children knew he would do exactly what he said he would do—pleasant or unpleasant. "Over the years," Billy recalls, "Paul has become a better parent, but the key to it has been consistency. He seems to develop every year more ability to do and say exactly the right thing to each one of us."

Billy's latest venture has been the building a new drag racing facility called the Texas Motorplex. He purchased five hundred acres of land south of Dallas, Texas, and constructed one of the nation's finest racing installations. Billy worked with the architects and planners to lay out the track and viewing facilities, put together the financing package, personally sold the advertising signs at the track, and arranged for sanctioned events and extensive television coverage. The Motorplex opened in the summer of 1986 and immediately attracted spectators, race drivers and income far in excess of projections. Racer car drivers have declared the track the best in the country and predict that all the new records in the next few years will be set on this track. The dream goal Billy has pursued for ten years has become a reality.

Billy is consciously following much of Paul's example as a father in the rearing of his own children, Adam and Christen Marie. "I guess the best proof that Dad's ideas about being a parent and about the real values in life are good is that all of us have gone through a period of rebellion of different kinds, testing the ideas he had taught us—but in the end we have all come back to the things he thought were important. We have found out that he was right all along." Billy feels fortunate that he has the advantage of having been taught good values. He is also grateful that his wife Deborah shares those values. Together they are designing their own personal style of parenting to give their children security based on a high self-image and a sense of what is right. Billy considers his marriage a partnership to which both he and Deborah contribute. Although they were both given high ideals by their parents, Deborah's life was more sheltered and structured by her parents than Billy's was. Since their marriage, Deborah has gained more self-reliance and is taking more personal responsibility for making her own choices. Billy has followed Deborah's lead in strengthening his spiritual life and tying it more closely to their church.

The latest of Paul's children to receive her "freedom" is Janna who just recently turned twenty-one. She is now experiencing the same initial searching through which the boys found their way when they were her age. She has not made a final decision about a career, but she has a job and is self-supporting.

One of Janna's experiences as a high school student illustrates both Paul's high expectations for his children and his support for them. Like many teen-agers, Janna loved to sleep late. For several years, her mother called her repeatedly in the morning, pushed her to eat breakfast, nagged her to get dressed, and drove her to school. Mornings were turning into a running battle that started the whole family's day with tension and cross tempers. Finally Paul sat down with Janna and his wife Jane for a problem-solving talk. The three concluded that a change was definitely needed and that Janna held the key to the solution. The result was a plan they all agreed to follow. Janna would set her alarm, get up without being called, and get ready for school. On days that she was ready by 8:00 a.m., Paul or Jane would drive her to school. On any day that she was not ready on time, she would get to school on her own and would be responsible for dealing with the consequences when she arrived late. Janna was glad to have Jane off her back. Jane and Paul were glad to have peace and quiet in the morning.

Janna's new plan worked well part of the time, but the old habit of sleeping late was hard to break. Some mornings Janna was up and ready on time; some days she was late. After several weeks, Paul received a call from the assistant principal's office asking him to come in for a conference. When he and Janna met with the assistant principal, her record of tardies was presented and Paul was asked what he intended to do about it. "Nothing," he said. That produced quite a shock. School officials were accustomed to hearing parents promise to push their children to do better. Paul refused to take responsibility for something he believed was Janna's business. "Do you have any other complaints about Janna?" Paul asked. There were none. "I think it's great that she has only one problem," Paul continued. "Janna is becoming a fine young woman. I believe she has her act at least 90% together. Being on time is one of the areas she hasn't quite mastered yet. But she has so many good qualities that I refuse to write her off as a bad job just because she still has one more area to work on. She'll solve the problem. If you have school rules about penalties for being tardy, she'll pay the penalty; and I'll support you in seeing that she does. But I refuse to take over her life and do something for her that she should be accepting personal responsibility to do for herself."

The youngest Meyer daughter, Leslie, is growing up in the Meyer traditions and already shows many of the same strengths and drives that characterize other family members. She and Paul regularly work together on her goals program, and she has an impressive list of ambitious goals achieved. She regularly sets top records in Girl Scout cookie sales and in money-making projects for her school. She is an honor student in her classes and is learning to play the piano. At the age of ten while on vacation with her parents in the Cayman Islands, she earned certification in scuba diving—the youngest person ever to be certified. She and Paul took a class in underwater photography and the family vacation condominium in the Caymans is now decorated with a number of spectacular photos of tropical sea creatures that are Leslie's work.

Leslie considers her father tops. She appreciates the time he makes to spend with her on a regular basis. They ride bikes, swim, and play tennis for outdoor fun, and play a variety of games and read together for quieter times. Leslie has a large measure of her father's positive expectancy and joy of life. Now that she is the only child left at home, she serves as the family alarm clock. She is an early riser because she is always eager to meet each new day's joys. She customarily gets up, dresses for school, makes up her bed, and stops by her parents' bedroom to say good morning on her way to the kitchen to fix her breakfast. Her cheery disposition is a true family treasure. Leslie is also learning about the real world. Like the older children, she has specific assigned chores that she performs as her part of contributing to the family's comfort and happiness, and she receives a modest allowance. She has learned to use part of her allowance for gifts, part for fun, and part for savings to be used for items in her goals program. So careful and methodical is she about her money that Paul once told a group of distributors to whom he was speaking about money management that they should follow her example. "She firmly believes," he said, "that if she doesn't save a part of her allowance every week, the day will come when she will be bankrupt."

Leslie has adopted her father's positive expectancy—but not just for her own ability to succeed. She also believes that her father can do anything. In 1984, she wrote in her personal goals book that she wanted to meet Vice President George Bush who is a personal friend of Paul. "You know him and can introduce me," she told Paul. When

The Meyer daughters—Janna and Leslie.

Leslie's goal accomplished: to meet President Ronald Reagan.

the Vice President came to Waco for an appearance at a local political rally, Leslie told her father she wanted to attend the rally. At the meeting, Bush saw Paul and came to speak to him; Paul was able to introduce Leslie to him. At home that night, Leslie told her father, "Now I have met the vice president. Next I want to meet the president. You can introduce me." So she wrote it in her goals book—and Paul groaned as he wrote it in his, too. It took two years, but he managed it, and Leslie is the proud possessor of a picture of herself and her parents standing with a beaming Ronald Reagan at a Dallas Republican luncheon for a small group of key supporters.

Leslie has made excellent use of the opportunity to travel all over the world. She is eager to accompany Paul and Jane on the various trips Paul must make in connection with the business. Her experiences include walking on the Great Wall of China, diving on the Great Barrier Reef off Australia and in the beautiful waters surrounding the Cayman Islands, swimming in the Pacific Ocean off the coast of Mexico, and being one of the guests of honor at numerous receptions in Japan. No matter how exciting the travel, Leslie keeps up with her school assignments and maintains her high grade level at Waco Christian School.

Paul Meyer is a good father-in-law as well as a good father. Jim's wife Anne, Larry's wife Lynn, and Bill's wife Deborah all appreciate the kind of relationship they have with him. He has love enough for all, is ready to support and encourage them, but never interferes in the families of his sons. He exhibits the same high expectations for his grandchildren that he has always had for his children, and he offers positive encouragement, praise for success, and acceptance and love at all times.

Paul and his wife Jane have a marriage that is in many respects ideal. Paul plans ahead for time he and Jane can spend together. No matter how pressing his business problems become, he never allows them to eclipse his family life. Paul and Jane take time to map out the major activities for each year. Then Paul fits his business schedule around those times. Frequently during the year, they review their family goals plan, and make any additions or adjustments they choose to make. While they share many interests and activities, they also have personal interests they feel free to pursue alone. Paul exerts strong family leadership, but is not autocratic. Jane feels that she is free to disagree with his ideas, to ask for a change in his plans, or to express her opinions. The key to their easy relationship is that they are both flexible. Both Jane and Paul enjoy entertaining in their home, but Paul leaves most of the details to Jane, who is a fabulous cook and decorator. When the party gets really big—like a reception for over a hundred Japanese salespeople who came to Waco for a convention—they divide the work of planning and making needed arrangements.

The Meyer secret to the building of relationships is the principle he learned from his mother: "Never look up to any person, and never look down on any person." Paul sees goodness in everyone and expects to be enriched by the contact with every person he meets—and he wants to contribute something of value to everyone he meets. The bottom line is love.

CHAPTER NINE

AS A MAN THINKETH. . .

If your attitudes include disbelief in yourself, fear, hesitancy, inner conflict, then life will give back to you disbelief, fear, hesitancy and conflict.

But if you draw your attitudes from the power of your faith, life will give you the fulfillment of your dreams and ambitions.

Paul J. Meyer

CHAPTER NINE

AS A MAN THINKETH. . .

THE TOTAL PERSON

Early in the 1970's, Paul Meyer wrote an article that was printed in a number of trade journals. Its title was *The Total Person Concept*. The central idea of the piece was that the way to make a company productive and successful was to begin with the people in the company, teach them to set and achieve goals, and then the company would automatically be right.

All of Meyer's programs include the *Plan of Action* volume designed to help the user set up a personal goals program in six areas of life: physical, mental, social, financial, spiritual, and family life. Program content makes frequent reference to the need for building a balanced life by setting and achieving goals in all of these six areas. Meyer frequently emphasizes to the distributor organization the necessity for each salesperson to become a "product of the product" by using the program and "Plan of Action" to set and achieve meaningful personal goals. It is not surprising that he follows this concept in his own life. He is the premier "product of the product." Paul's own personal plan of action has long since outgrown the confines of a single notebook. He has a three-ring binder for each area of life, and in addition, makes a separate plan of action binder for each major project he undertakes. For example, since he has been investing in real estate on a large scale, he has followed the practice of making a plan of action for each piece of property he purchases. This volume is regularly updated with information on the progress of its operation; and when the time comes to sell the property, every applicable piece of information is at hand. He is just as methodical in every area of life.

Physical. At the age of forty-five, Paul Meyer decided to take up tennis, a sport he had never before played. Up until this age, he had enjoyed playing basketball in the Waco city league. Some trouble with his knees led him to choose a new sport that would provide excellent exercise and the opportunity to compete while cutting down a little on the necessary running. Tennis seemed the best choice. In typical Meyer fashion, Paul decided he would become a Class A tennis player. Almost as soon as he owned a tennis racquet, he hung an attractive wall plaque in his office that declared "I am a Class A tennis player." He decided that the proof this goal had been achieved would be gaining state ranking in his age group. After considering all the work this would take, he concluded that he would set a ten-year target date for achievement of the goal. Then he developed his plan—in a thick binder devoted exclusively to the project.

Achievement of his goal, Paul knew, would require new attitudes, new physical habits, development of new skills, and specific activities. His wall plaque affirmation was just a beginning of the devices he used to build new attitudes. He subscribed to tennis magazines and began to read them regularly. He started watching tennis matches on television at every opportunity. He visited a pro shop and asked about equipment, then purchased racquets, balls, and tennis clothes. To develop the needed new skills, he began taking tennis lessons on a regular schedule and followed the advice of the tennis pro about practice with the ball machine and on the backboard, and finally with opponents. He even went to tennis camps and seminars run by top pros all over the country. One of these pros told him that to become any good at tennis, he would have to spend twice as many hours of work and practice as the average player his age spent if he wanted to catch up with those who had been playing for twenty-five years or longer. There could be no short cuts. Paul was determined to succeed; so he made the time for practice.

As he learned the basics of the game, Paul began to pick out people he saw on the court as possible opponents. He chose three or four at a time and set a goal to beat them during the next three months. When he could finally beat each of them on a fairly regular basis, he chose three or four new players who were a little bit better, and set out to defeat them. Almost before he could believe it possible, he was winning over most of the Waco players in his age group. Then came the time for tournament play. His goal to achieve state ranking in his age group was achieved only seven years after he started playing—three years ahead of schedule. Since that time, he has been ranked in the state every year.

Paul complains with mock seriousness that tennis has cost him thousands and thousands of dollars as well as untold hard work and numerous adjustments to new conditions in his life. As he concentrated on developing his tennis skills, he decided it would be great to have a tennis court in his own back yard. That would save him lots of time and add to his ability to entertain his tennis friends. There was only one problem: his back yard sloped steeply down to the lakeside. There was not a level space large enough to build a court. He hired some engineers to tell him what could be done. They produced a plan for sinking piers and building the court on a cantilevered platform, but the unstable ground conditions made it almost certain that the platform would develop serious cracks. In addition, it would probably cost close to half a million dollars. But Paul J. Meyer never gives up! He did not abandon his goal, but he did put it on hold for a while. Then one day a woman showed up at his front door and said she wanted to buy his house. When he protested that it was not for sale, she insisted. "I know just the house for you in place of this one," she urged. "It has lots of room for a tennis court." Almost before the family knew what was happening, they were surrounded by boxes and crates—all ready to move. As part of settling into their new home, Paul had a tennis court built.

But the story goes on! When Paul consciously postpones a goal, it seems to gain momentum rather than coming to a halt. About the same time he bought the new home, a small tennis club to which the family belonged was put up for sale. It appeared that a possible buyer would close a deal—and the club. Paul thought it would be a shame for Waco to lose this nice family facility; so he bought the club—and its eleven tennis courts. "Be careful what goal you set," Paul warns; "for that is surely what you will get." And he illustrates that truth with the story about how he acquired not one, but twelve tennis courts. "When you set goals," he often says, "success comes like bananas—in bunches."

Paul's physical goals program has changed his life in a number of ways. His diet has changed over the last decade as he has studied all the best available information on nutrition. He has almost entirely eliminated beef and pork from his diet, relying on fish and chicken for most of his protein. He has increased the fresh fruit and vegetable content in his diet and cut down on both sugar and salt. He follows a regular program of exercise and has regular check ups to monitor all the signs of fitness. His careful health regimen has resulted in a gradual reduction of weight as recommended for men in the middle years, and yearly reduction in cholesterol and triglyceride levels.

Mental. Meyer continues his life-long habit of wide and varied reading. He regularly reads a large number of newspapers and business periodicals as well as a wide sampling of new books in his areas of interest. He and daughter Leslie also spend regular time memorizing scripture. The morning drive to school is one of their favorite times to practice saying the verses on which they are currently working. Paul confesses that he sometimes feels a little jealous when he sees how quickly and effortlessly Leslie memorizes compared to the effort he spends to accomplish the same goal.

Social. Paul Meyer's consuming interest in people and belief in the innate worth of all people gives him a social ease that allows him to discover common ground with almost anyone he meets. His curiosity and his genuine concern for others make it impossible for him to spend more than five minutes with someone else without uncovering some interesting information that can serve as a basis for interaction. He and Jane have a wide circle of friends they enjoy entertaining, meeting for lunch or dinner, or for a game of tennis, or other outing. They frequently attend the Baylor University or Dallas Cowboys football games in their motor coach, inviting friends they see in the stands to join them for coffee and snacks at half time.

Financial. Paul Meyer's financial goals are probably the most structured of all his goals. But even these goals are marked by flexibility and strictly governed by his personal values. He believes in setting goals for earnings, for meeting necessary expenses, for savings, and for investment. He maintains an overall long-range plan for earnings with specific, detailed plans for the first year of that long-range plan. Each year he updates his long-range plan by making a more detailed annual plan for the new year and adding to the future of the long-range plan. Because his financial holdings are complex, he retains the services of top-flight experts to advise him on accounting and tax matters. He knows that such affairs cannot be left to chance. In addition to the overall plan, Paul has separate financial plans for each segment of his financial holdings with budgets, *pro forma* statements, action steps to be taken, and plans for overcoming any obstacles that he anticipates.

Paul Meyer believes strongly in conducting all his affairs—including his financial affairs—in strict conformity with his personal values and standards. His basic guiding principle in financial matters is always the Golden Rule: "Do unto others as you would have them do unto you." He recognizes the fact that success in business requires hard decisions and sometimes means paying out money now to earn some future profit. But he rejects utterly the idea that for one person to earn a profit another must suffer a loss. He refuses to do business on that basis, preferring, instead, to look for a course of action that will benefit every party involved. So strictly does he follow the Golden Rule that he often passes up an opportunity for personal profit that would cause hardship or loss for someone else. He prefers to wait until a way can be found for a Win/Win transaction to take place.

When Meyer sells a piece of real estate, he has all the numbers available—and he freely shares them with the prospective purchaser before the sale is concluded. Lenders enjoy doing business with him because they know there will be no surprises in connection with any of their deals. One local banker recently remarked that he had never done business with anyone who kept better records and had more information immediately available than Meyer.

Spiritual. Part of Paul Meyer's heritage is the importance he places on the spiritual part of life—an attitude he adopted from observing the daily conduct of his mother. It was natural for her to speak of God's work in the world and in the lives of people, for she knew His presence in her own life. Paul's spiritual commitment has been an important factor in all of his adult life, but it has become even more important over the last ten years. The excitement and flamboyant life style that marked his success in his twenties was replaced in his thirties by hard work and intensity in building his company. By the time he reached the mid-forties, there was time available to slow down and reflect on the meaning of all that had taken place. The three Meyer sons were grown and on their own; so family life was quieter and less complicated by the sheer force of numbers. The company was well on its way to stability and success; competent officers were at the head of each portion of the work, and less of Paul's day-to-day attention to detail was required. His personal income had continued to climb and he had added resources to use in any project that attracted him.

Over the last ten years, Paul has made a conscious effort to become more involved in the active exercise of his Christian commitment

Paul dives with daughter Leslie—the youngest person to qualify in Cayman Islands for scuba diving.

Paul's daughter Janna.

Paul and wife Jane.

through service in his church, through Christian stewardship, and through openly acknowledging his personal faith in God. One of the effects of this effort has been the gradual increase in the emphasis on values and spiritual needs in SMI materials. Because SMI programs are designed for use by all kinds of people, it is not appropriate that specific theological positions be presented. Meyer believes, however, that it is highly proper to encourage people to face the spiritual area of life and to come to terms with their own spiritual needs as one part of planning for personal effectiveness and success.

When Meyer traveled to Japan in 1984 for the convention of the company's Japanese salespeople, he was scheduled to make the key address. This convention marked some significant changes in the Japanese business. The new company name, PJM Japan, Ltd., had just been adopted; Hei Arita had just been made head of the entire Japanese operation; and new Japanese programs were being introduced. Paul believed this was an opportunity for him to share with the Japanese salespeople some of his own values and beliefs. At the end of his speech, Paul appealed to all of the people associated with the company to consider the importance of becoming well-rounded in all areas of their lives by setting and achieving goals that were personally appropriate. He concluded by telling the audience that he especially wanted them to consider the importance of the spiritual area of life, adding that he was personally a Christian and invited them to consider the Christian way of life and decide whether it might fill their spiritual needs as it has filled his. His willingness to share his personal beliefs made a strong impression on those who heard him.

Family life. His family are the most important people in Paul Meyer's life. In addition to planning ahead for big events like vacations, he makes small bits of time available on a daily basis for enjoying their company. Paul has his main working office in a separate wing of his home although he also maintains an office at company headquarters. This arrangement makes it easy for him to take a break for a brief conversation with Jane, to say hello to Leslie's friends who come home with her from school, or to step out to the tennis court and watch his grandsons hit a few balls. When Leslie was just a toddler, she often brought a doll or some building blocks to his office and sat quietly in a corner just to be near him. Not long ago, one of the company officers came for a conference with Paul and found Adam,

We are either the masters or the victims of our attitudes.

It's a matter of personal choice — blessing or curse.

Paul J. Meyer

Billy's small son, sitting in Paul's lap watching in fascination as his grandfather made telephone calls.

The extended Meyer family forms a close-knit group. They often gather for dinner and an evening at home with nothing special planned except to enjoy one another's company. It is not unusual on these evenings for Paul to disappear from the family room. When someone looks for him, he is most likely to be found sitting on the floor in the play room playing with one or more of the grandchildren.

ROLE MODELS

No one understands better than Paul Meyer the importance of the influence one person can have on another. He recognizes with gratitude the debt he owes to a number of people who have influenced his life; he also accepts personal responsibility for making his own choice of the models he has followed. Both the debt and the choice can be seen in the characteristics he has adopted from both his parents. Paul Meyer's staunch Christian faith and his innate sense of fairness can be traced to the influence of his mother. Her love of knowledge and her belief in people are also traits he learned from her. From his father, Paul learned resourcefulness, determination, persistence, and pride in a job well done. From his father he also learned thrift, the importance of saving and investing his money, and the value of hard work.

A variety of other people have exerted significant influence on Paul Meyer—probably without being conscious of doing so:

W. Clement Stone: Early in his career, Paul adopted Mr. Stone as something of a hero. He admired his keen business sense and his skill in making money. Even more, he admired his compassion, love and concern for people and his demonstration of the joy of giving through his many benevolent and philanthropic projects.

Lee Boswell: When Paul was a young insurance agent in Florida, Mr. Boswell was one of his clients. He was one of the most successful people Paul had ever known. His personal wealth came from ownership of large orange groves and stock holdings in insurance companies. What impressed Paul most, however, was Mr. Boswell's practice of buying businesses that were about to become bankrupt just to save the jobs of the employees. He would then work very hard to get the business back on its feet, and making a profit. Although Mr. Boswell was extremely rich, he lived modestly. He was an extraordinary example of a giving person. Paul considered him an outstanding Christian businessman and an excellent father and wanted to be like him.

Bill Hinson: Paul and Bill became friends when Bill was the pastor of the church Paul attended in Florida. He helped Paul weather storms when facing reverses and adjust to affluence when things were going well. The two have remained friends over the years and continue to encourage one another and just to enjoy being together when they can. Bill often serves as a sounding board for Paul's ideas about using Christian principles in his business activities.

J. Clifton Williams: Clif Williams is now a professor of management in the Hankamer School of Business at Baylor University. For several years he was associated with SMI and, during this time, wrote two of the first business programs that SMI produced. With the addition of Paul's goal setting materials and *Plan of Action,* these programs have benefited thousands of companies and managers over the years. Paul first observed Clif's strong Christian value system when Clif was the teacher of the Sunday School class Paul attended. His admiration grew as he observed in Clif the possibility of a practical application of such a value system in the business world. Clif's example has helped Paul feel sure about the rightness of the ethical principles he has chosen to follow in his own business and to feel secure in including in his programs emphasis on the need for establishing personal values and goals in all areas of life.

J.B. King: Mr. King was Paul's father-in-law. He helped Paul get his very first job selling weekly premium insurance. Paul remembers Mr. King as a true "Southern Gentleman." He was a loving and giving person, a strong influence on Paul at the time he was just beginning his own career.

Bernard Rapoport: Mr. Rapoport is the founder and president of the American Income Life Insurance Company, whose home office is in Waco. Paul met him soon after he moved to Waco and immediately learned to respect him. He was particularly impressed with Mr. Rapoport's generosity as a charitable giver and has used him as a model for his own benevolent activities.

Chuck Williams: Chuck has influenced the whole company from an ethical standpoint. Paul especially admires Chuck's combination of good business sense and his keen knowledge of the Bible. He is a tireless worker in performance of his company responsibilities, but he reserves time for scripture study and for teaching a Bible class in his church. Paul attended his class for a period of five years. Paul often calls on Chuck for his opinion about spiritual matters as they affect the business and also as they affect his personal life and relationships.

Gladys Hudson: As president of Success Motivation, Inc., Gladys has worked with Paul in research and development of new products and revision and updating of older programs. Her strong Christian value system and ethical standards have encouraged Paul to include in the programs more specific material relating to values and to give more verbal expression to his own spiritual values and commitment.

COMMITMENT TO CHRISTIAN STEWARDSHIP

From the day that the youthful Paul Meyer, harvesting fruit in a California orchard, vowed he would earn his living by using his mind instead of his hands, he has been determined that he would be wealthy—perhaps partly as insurance against the need for that kind of work. Paul's greatest joy in his wealth, however, is in giving it away. Although his family lives comfortably, travels when desired, and enjoys many comforts, there is no wanton waste in the Meyer household. There are no wild shopping sprees to buy clothes or jewelry that is never worn; purchases are not always the "biggest and the best" just because the money is available. When Leslie expressed a desire to learn to play the piano, she was given a small spinet. Just recently the family decided to trade the spinet for a grand piano. Leslie was excited about having a grand piano. But they chose a baby grand—not the more expensive concert grand. Later, Paul promised Leslie, the baby grand will be traded for a concert grand if her interest in the piano continues and she plays well enough to gain real benefit from owning the larger instrument.

Few people have opportunity to see the extent of Paul's philanthropic activities. Many of the business people in Waco know that they are likely to receive a call from Paul several times a year asking for contributions to one cause or another, but most of them never stop to realize that he has personally given many times the amount he asks them to promise. Paul's first stewardship obligation is to his church, and he follows a regular plan of scriptural giving. Outside of his church, most of Paul's gifts go to youth organizations, for scholarships, to education, and to Christian missions. He sees in these causes not only a chance to help people today, but an opportunity to affect the future.

One of Paul's favorite projects is the Waco Boys' Club. He first became interested in this organization soon after he had founded SMI. One Sunday in the early 1960's as he was leaving church, Floyd Casey, an older man in the church, walked up beside Paul, put his arm around Paul's shoulder and said, "Paul, I've been watching you. I believe your company is going to be a big success. You're working very hard in it now, but the time will come when you will have more time for yourself, as well as plenty of money. When that time comes, you will need something that will give greater meaning to your life. I hope you will take a look at the Waco Boys' Club and see whether it could fill that need for you." Paul looked; and he liked what he saw. The Boys' Club ministers to several thousand children in Waco, most of them from low income or disadvantaged families. The Club was actively producing good citizens, young people with high ideals and a desire to achieve.

Paul became an active benefactor of the Boys' Club, and soon was elected to its Board of Directors. Under his influence, the Boys' Club has developed a goals program dealing with facilities, operating personnel, programs, and equipment. Several of SMI's officers have also been active in Boys' Club matters. Chuck Williams, Jim Sirbasku, Gene Franklin, and L.D. Tanner have been especially interested in the project, and they have worked with the Board of Directors and the operating personnel of the Boys' Club to develop and operate a complete goals program. Paul has helped to plan and implement fund-raising programs that have built a swimming pool, renovated the main club building, and provided for expansion facilities into two additional locations. In the process of working on Boys' Club projects, Paul has formed especially close friendships with Waco businessmen Joe Brownfield, F.M. Young, and Weldon Youngblood, all of whom have been major contributors to the Club. In 1983, the Waco Boys' Club Foundation was established to build a permanent endowment fund for the future operation of the club. In 1985, in recognition of his outstanding service to the Waco Boys' Club, Paul was given the Boys' Club Medallion by the Boys' Clubs of America, the highest honor given to any laymen by the national organization. This award was presented in recognition of Meyer's outstanding contributions to the Waco Club through promotion of the fund-raising campaign and the formation of a new branch location of the Boys' Club in Waco.

Because of the lasting impression his own scouting days made on his life, Paul Meyer has always been a strong supporter of the Scouts. He is a major supporter of the Heart of Texas Council of the Boy Scouts of America. Most of Paul's involvement with scouting is in fund raising, long-range planning, and goal setting. His expertise in the area of goal setting has helped the HOT Council move faster and operate more efficiently than it might otherwise have done. Under his influence, the Council decided to develop a full goals program. Paul recruited Chuck Williams to lead in this project. His service to the Council was so valuable that Chuck was asked to become a member of the Council and in 1985 was elected president of the Council. In 1981, the Boy Scouts of America made Meyer a Distinguished Eagle Scout. This award, which is given only to men who were Eagle Scouts in their youth, recognizes outstanding service to youth and to the Boy Scout organization. Especially coveted because it is given so rarely, the Distinguished Eagle Scout award has been given to such noted figures as former President Gerald Ford, astronaut John Glenn, and former Texas Governor William Clements.

Outside of his church—the First Baptist Church of Woodway—one of the major beneficiaries of Paul's stewardship is the Haggai Institute of Advanced Leadership Training. This organization, founded by John Haggai, operates a training school in Singapore for Christian leaders from Third World nations. The purpose is to train these people in the techniques of evangelism and leadership so that they may, in turn, train other leaders in their own countries and serve along with these additional trained leaders in the active evangelization of their people. The goal of the Haggai Institute is, by the year 2000, to train ten thousand credentialed third world leaders who will, in turn, train an additional one million leaders for the all-important work of evangelism. Meyer is a member of the Board of Trustees of the Institute, which has its administrative headquarters in Atlanta, Georgia.

Paul first heard of John Haggai's work through Bill Hinson, who thought the two had many qualities in common. Paul was immediately attracted by the concept of the Haggai organization. He recognized its practical approach through multiplying the efforts of Haggai himself and of each trainee who attended the training sessions in Singapore. Using Christian leaders who are people of stature and ability to reach people in their own cultures seemed to him the fastest way to do effective mission work. Meyer and Haggai began to correspond and to talk frequently by telephone, but for several years they did not meet in person. One day in 1969, Paul was walking through a hotel in San Francisco, passed a meeting room, and heard a familiar voice. "That has to be John Haggai," Paul told himself. He went into the room and listened to the remainder of the speech. He was right. It was John Haggai. Since that time, the two have developed a close friendship, and Meyer has become a significant contributor to the work of Haggai Institute.

Bill Hinson not only told Paul about John Haggai, he told John about Paul. John was especially impressed with Bill Hinson's description of Meyer's commitment to using his time by priorities. "He doesn't go to bed until he has scheduled the next day's activities—even if it is 2:00 a.m.," Bill related. When Meyer and Haggai finally met, they became fast friends. "I have followed his life, career, and Christian odyssey with fascination and benefit," Haggai remembers. "By most standards, he is a paradox. He has made millions, but he is not a money-grabbing materialist; he gives a phenomenal percentage of his income to outside causes. The master of time management, he drops everything to counsel someone in a crisis. A master of anticipating obstacles, he never blames others when things go wrong. Called insensitive by some, he astounds all who know him by the lightning speed with which he asks and grants forgiveness. He walks with ease among leaders from every stratum of society, every level of intelligence and education, every rank of business, every brand of religion—yet reserves time every day for prayer and Bible study, both personally and with his family. His master goal is to do God's will. And in the doing of it, he helps other people reach their potential. He is the consummate 'encourager.'"

In typical Meyer fashion, however, money is only one part of Paul's contribution to the Haggai Institute. He has, with the help of Chuck Williams, led the Institute to set up a long-range goals program that is already making a significant impact on the growth and effectiveness of its work. One outcome of the development of the goals program is the decision to open a second training facility in Hawaii to supplement the work of the Singapore campus. As the goals program was being developed, a part of the process was to determine how many leaders must be trained each year if the goal of training ten thousand leaders by the year 2000 were to be achieved. When that number was projected, it was obvious that the Singapore campus would not accommodate this volume of trainees. The choice was made to open a second facility rather than to try to expand the existing campus. The new facility will be built in Hawaii. Land has already been acquired, and the new buildings will soon be ready for occupancy. Personnel to operate the new campus are already being recruited and trained.

In July, 1980, the Haggai Institute for Advanced Leadership Training recognized Meyer's outstanding contributions to its work by presenting to him a special award and citation.

Paul Meyer's interest in young people inevitably led him to an interest in education. For several years he served on the Board of Trustees of the Vanguard College Preparatory School in Waco. During his term of service, he assisted in raising funds to build a new gymnasium for the school—with an interesting addition to the story of his "tennis court" acquisitions. To help finance the gymnasium, Paul and Jim Mathis organized an indoor tennis club made up of a number of Waco businessmen in his age group who agreed to give a specified sum of money toward construction of the gym and then to pay club dues to be used for upkeep of the gym. In return, they had the privilege of playing on the indoor tennis court in the new gym at hours when students would not be using it. Since Waco had no indoor tennis courts anywhere else, Paul used this "selling benefit" in his fund-raising presentation. "Show people how they will benefit," Paul says, "and they sell

Excerpt from Paul J. Meyer's *Charitable Plan of Action*

Purpose—Reason for Giving
It Is More Blessed to Give than to Receive

"For unto whomsoever much is given of him shall be much required."

Luke 12:48

"Material gain, in and of itself, is a dead end and a loser's road. Wealth or money is just an extension of your personality. That is a gift that comes from God. It should be like all other talent—the more you pour out, the more you have to pour—the more you give, the more you have to give—the more you share, the more you have to share."

Paul J. Meyer, Sr.

"The purpose of living is to give, to share, and to multiply yourself mentally, spiritually, and materially."

Paul J. Meyer, Sr.

"As ye would that men should do to you, do ye also to them."

Luke 6:31

"We bring nothing into this world. We take nothing out. We are stewards of what we have or accumulate.

Paul J. Meyer, Sr.

"I know how to get along with humble means, and I also know how to live in prosperity; in any and every circumstance I have learned the secret of being filled and going hungry, both of having abundance and suffering need. I can do all things through Him who strengthens me."

Phil. 4:12, 13

"Give, and it will be given unto you: good measure, pressed down, shaken together and running over will be put into your bosom. For with the same measure that you use, it will be measured back to you.

Luke 6:38

themselves." It works in benevolence, in selling insurance, or in selling SMI programs. Meyer is also an active supporter of Baylor University in Waco, Texas. He has recently made a pledge for a gift of $2,000,00.00 to be given over a period of two years that will go toward the cost of building a special events center on the campus.

Waco Christian School, where Leslie is a student, has become an important focus of Meyer's interest in quality education. He helped the school in a fund-raising drive to provide money for construction of several new classrooms and a gymnasium, which is now completed. Leslie is following in her father's footsteps. When the school's students participate in fund-raising events through selling Christmas candles or magazine subscriptions, Leslie is always one of the top salespeople When she was in the fourth grade, the students held a school Olympics. Each student secured sponsors who agreed to give a certain amount for each lap that student ran in the time limit set for the event. Leslie secured an impressive list of sponsors—all on her own. She did not ask her father to help.

Paul Meyer's interest in youth and in the need for young people to reach their full potential is expressed in his generous program of scholarship support for various young people whose needs come to his attention. Students in six different schools and colleges are currently receiving full or partial support for tuition and other school expenses through Meyer's gifts. When he gives scholarship help, Meyer gives more than money. He keeps in close touch with all of the scholarship students so that he knows about their plans, their progress, and any other needs they have. He encourages them to accept responsibility for developing their full potential first, through education, but also through planning and looking ahead to a future of success and achievement.

To perpetuate his ability to give to the benevolent causes that interest him, Paul has formed the Paul J. Meyer Family Foundation. He is building the assets of the Foundation so that a permanent source of income will exist to give continued support to various charitable groups.

In the usual Meyer custom, Paul has a separate *Charitable Plan of Action.* In it are long- and short-range goals with complete plans for their achievement, progress reports on those that are underway, and action steps that are still to be taken—all planned out with target dates and what source of funds will be used. But of major interest to one who would understand what makes someone undertake such a pro-

The only honest
measure
of your success
is what you are doing
compared to
your true
potential.

Paul J. Meyer

gram is the first page in this *Plan of Action:* a statement of Paul's personal reasons for giving that provides an insight into his beliefs and value system.

A LOOK TO THE FUTURE

Paul Meyer's goal for the last half of the 1980's is to "uncomplicate" his life. He has already been making plans for this process for a number of years, and his investment of time and effort is now paying dividends.

Once Paul took Henry Tseung's advice to start delegating, he rapidly became a master of the art. As a result, he has been slowly working himself out of a job in the company. Here is the plan he follows:

1. Each company has a president in charge. Once a month, each president submits a president's report to Meyer. This one-page report lists the greatest problem of the company, what the president intends to do to solve it, and a "recap" of the results achieved the past month.
2. A monthly computer print-out goes to Meyer, comparing the actual results to goals, to last year, and to the budget.
3. Once a month Meyer meets with each president or other key person to review the president's report and the computer reports. This meeting maintains the bond of unity, trust, and respect that exists in the organization.
4. An annual goals program is written for each division and company and then compiled into a master goals program that is used as the basis of evaluating the progress of each division, company, and officer.
5. The organization is structured to provide multiple pockets of leadership so that growth can be accommodated. Each segment of the business must pull its own weight. Paul demands that "each keg stand on its own bottom." Each part of the organization also has built-in methods for measuring its performance. Paul believes that "if you can't measure it, you can't manage it." The key is concentration on the personal growth of key executives. When individuals grow, the whole company benefits.

Goals accomplished: flying a glider. . .

. . . and riding in a hot air balloon.

Meyer has deliberately built a corporate environment that attracts people with the entrepreneurial spirit. Executives are compensated by salary, commission, bonus and profit sharing—all designed to fit the goals of the company and of the individuals involved. His foresight is paying off as strong executives assume more and more responsibility for planning and operation, giving Paul the freedom to control policy and general direction, confident that the executives he has gathered around him will follow them.

Part of his plan to uncomplicate his life is Paul's new vacation condominium in the Cayman Islands. Paul, Jane, and Leslie regularly spend several long periods of time each year enjoying the relaxed life style, the sunshine, and the water. Paul has decided that modern technology is great. From his office, with the help of long distance telephone and a facsimile machine, he can be in instant touch with the Waco office or with anyone in the world organization. The real bonus Paul has discovered is that many people still stand somewhat in awe of these technical devices. As a result, they tend to solve their own problems instead of bringing them to Paul as they do when he seems more easily accessible. This arrangement frees Paul from nagging details; but the most important effect is that people learn to exercise initiative, to make decisions, and to solve problems on their own—to become stronger and more successful.

Paul Meyer's concept of uncomplicating his life might not be what a lot of people would expect. His list of new goals for the future is both challenging and exciting. His main purpose is to continue to grow in all six areas of life: physical, mental, social, spiritual, financial, and family life. He is especially eager to grow in his Christian pilgrimage by using his talents, skills, and knowledge to help other people. One of his firm priorities is to continue using his money-making talent and skills so that he can expand his program of charitable giving and increase his ability to give. The Paul J. Meyer Family Foundation is the major vehicle he is using to insure a permanent income that will make his giving last far beyond his lifetime.

In his business, Meyer plans to continue on the same track of success, to continue to expand the company's markets and services, and to motivate greater numbers of people to use their full potential.

Meyer has noticed that too many people who retire from their active business also retire from other aspects of life. He plans to continue learning and growing. He will continue his long-time practice of enhancing his vocabulary, and he intends to remain physically active, also. His list of goals includes learning to hang glide—he already knows where he will learn how—and scuba diving in the Red Sea. He has plans to visit twenty countries that he has not yet seen. His most "far out" goal—in more than one sense—is to make a space flight. Characteristically, this is more than an idle dream. Paul already has made a reservation and paid a deposit on a ticket for one of the first space flights that will carry commercial travelers—flights scheduled to begin in 1992.

LEGACY TO HIS FAMILY

When Paul Meyer thinks about leaving a legacy to his children, he turns instinctively to intangibles rather than to money. He considers the value of the heritage he received from his parents, and he hopes to give his own children the character traits and attitudes that are far more valuable than money.

Faith in God. Paul's faith has seen him through both hard times and prosperity. He actively practices his faith and gives his children the opportunity to see the importance in his life of his belief in God.

A positive attitude. All their lives, the Meyer children have been encouraged to think positively about seizing opportunities, overcoming obstacles, and achieving their dreams. Paul continues to maintain his own positive attitude about the future as well as the present as an example for his children to see that every stage of life presents challenges and opportunities for success and achievement.

High self-image. Paul Meyer is a strong believer in the importance of having a high self-image. He believes that God made each human being unique so that each one could achieve in a personal way. Each one must fulfill the role God gives him, and each one, then, can feel a sense of personal worth while pursuing God's purpose for his life. He makes it a habit to reinforce the positive traits he observes in his children, to give praise when it is deserved, and to express unconditional love for each one.

Honesty and integrity. Because God has placed us in a world of such abundance, there is plenty for all. Meyer conducts his own business dealings with strict honesty and integrity. He agrees wholeheartedly with the wise man who wrote in Proverbs 19:1, "Better be poor and above reproach than rich and crooked in speech."

Love of giving. Paul Meyer often says that there are two kinds of people in the world: takers and givers. He has tried to teach his children by both word and example to be givers. He wants his children to be giving in personal relationships as well as in stewardship of their possessions. He believes that a gift of money offered grudgingly and without love is worse than no gift at all.

Practice of goal setting. Each of the Meyer children has been taught to understand and practice goal setting. Paul hopes that his teaching and his example will stay with them throughout their lives. High principles and sound values are vital; but without challenging goals, principles and values have no avenue for expression. His hope is that he will inspire in his children what he purposed to do for other people and expressed in his company's slogan: "motivating people to their full potential." No greater goal is possible than for one to attain all that God has made possible.

AS A MAN THINKETH. . .

We are told that God looks primarily at a man's heart. But we can look only at a man's deeds to learn what is in his heart. The Bible tells us that "as a man thinketh in his heart, so is he." Since thoughts are translated into actions, we can see—at least in part—the nature of Paul Meyer's heart: belief in people and love for them, commitment to a purpose for his life, determination to be all he can be—all undergirded by a vibrant faith in God and commitment to an active stewardship of all the gifts God has given him.

SMI International, Inc.

The most valuable asset any individual possesses is a unique, innate God-given potential for achievement and success. The most important asset of any company or organization is the unrecognized or unused potential of its people for creative productivity.

SMI International's primary goal is to provide materials that will help people discover and use more of the potential they already possess. Most people have more knowledge, skills and ability than they use. Many psychologists have estimated that most people use less than 30% of their mental capacity. The remainder lies dormant from a lack of motivation.

The programs offered by SMI International have proved to be outstanding tools that people can use to design for themselves ways to use more of their potential, to build an unending source of motivation, and to bring their dreams into reality.

In addition to giving individuals the tools of success, SMI International programs are effective when used in organizational groups. When people learn new motivational concepts and acquire skills that enhance organizational performance, the goals of the organization move from the realm of uncertain projection into the reality of measurable achievement. Programs available address these areas:

Leadership and personal growth

Sales skills

Sales management

Communication skills

Personal motivation

Personal and organizational time management

Supervisory skills

SMI International offers exciting options for people who are dissatisfied with the direction their lives seem to be moving. For information about how SMI International can serve you or your organization, write or call:

SMI International, Inc.
P.O. Box 2506
Waco, Texas 76702–2506
Telephone: 1–800–433–1003